THE TERRITORIAL DIVISIONS

THE TERRITORIAL DIVISIONS

1914-1918

BY

J. STIRLING
LATE MAJOR
8TH BATT. ROYAL SCOTS

The Naval & Military Press Ltd

Published by

The Naval & Military Press Ltd
Unit 5 Riverside, Brambleside
Bellbrook Industrial Estate
Uckfield, East Sussex
TN22 1QQ England

Tel: +44 (0)1825 749494

www.naval-military-press.com
www.nmarchive.com

Cover image:
Lancashire Fusiliers of the 125th Brigade, 42nd (East Lancashire) Division, bound for Cape Helles, Gallipoli, May 1915. The soldiers have just disembarked aboard *Trawler 318* from the transport *SS Nile*, from the deck of which the photo was taken.

In reprinting in facsimile from the original, any imperfections are inevitably reproduced and the quality may fall short of modern type and cartographic standards.

INTRODUCTION

These Notes are composed very largely of extracts, relating to the work of Territorial Infantry Divisions, taken from the published despatches. These divisions saw a great deal of heavy fighting throughout the years 1916 and 1917, but the numbers, or Territorial designations, of formations operating on the Western Front were not given in despatches, as published in the *Gazette*, until the Commander-in-Chief reported on 20th February, 1918, as to the battle of Cambrai, November 1917. However, in the edition of *Sir Douglas Haig's Despatches*, published by Messrs. Dent, the divisions, which are referred to as being engaged in the more important battles, are identified by number; and, in compiling these Notes, advantage (with permission) has been taken of this additional information.

The facts recited by the Field-Marshals and Generals, who commanded the British Armies in the field, and the judgments expressed by them in their despatches seem to be the best, if not the only reliable, material from which to form an opinion on the value of the services of the Territorial Force in the great struggle. It will generally be admitted that the opinion of units on their own doings would

vi THE TERRITORIAL DIVISIONS

not be quite impartial and could not be used to form a basis for assessing the value of the Force as a whole.

Under the Territorial Act of 1907 fourteen infantry divisions were formed. Some of these sailed for the East in September and October, 1914, and all the fourteen had embarked for abroad before July 1915. If it had not been necessary to keep in view the question of armament and the possibility of invasion, several divisions might have been in France before the close of the first battle of Ypres. If that had been found practicable Lord French might have had fewer anxieties in November 1914. His Lordship, in his despatches and elsewhere, has borne testimony to the valuable services of the Territorial battalions which were under his command in 1914.

It is doubtful if Britain ever quite realised what it owed to the Territorials who went abroad before the New Armies were ready. Apart from the four divisions which went to the East in the autumn of 1914, thus allowing the Indian Corps to be brought to France, the Territorial strength, in France alone, in April 1915, before the second great struggle at Ypres broke out, probably exceeded that of the British Army at Mons, and it is by no means certain that the ten Regular divisions plus two Indian divisions and one Canadian could have held the great "gas attack."

In September 1914 the Army Council decided to

INTRODUCTION vii

raise second line units to take the place of those which had gone or were to go abroad. Before the end of that year most counties had raised their second lines, and in many, third line, or depot battalions to supply drafts had been recruited. The original function of the second line divisions was to form an army for use in the event of invasion being attempted, but, eventually, eight of these divisions went to active service abroad, chiefly in 1916; and one division of infantry, the 74th, was formed in the East, mainly from dismounted Yeomanry, and acquitted itself with credit in Palestine and afterwards in France. From those second line divisions which were not sent abroad some individual battalions were taken and all " A " category men remaining went as drafts.

Several of the second line divisions did extremely well, perhaps because they had the advantage of a long mobilised training at home before embarking, and the brotherhood or family spirit among all ranks was thoroughly developed. The original Territorial Force was doubtless deficient in many respects, but it started on mobilisation with the enormous advantage that the officers, N.C.O.s and men of a battalion were known to one another and the family spirit grew quickly.

During the first four months of the War, as already stated, many Territorial battalions went to the Front and were attached to Regular divisions;

some of these rejoined the Territorial divisions from their own districts when the latter arrived in the battle area; others were never in Territorial formations, serving throughout the War with the Regular or New Armies. No account of the doings of these latter battalions is given in these Notes, although some of the very best units in the Force were among those which never served in it at the Front. The value of their services, which was enhanced because they were able to go abroad at a most critical period, should not be forgotten.

The *Croix de Guerre* (*Palme en Bronze*), a coveted but seldom bestowed honour, was awarded by the President of the French Republic to one such battalion, the 4th, The King's Shropshire Light Infantry, T.F., in the following circumstances, as set out in the orders of the General commanding one of the French Armies:

" On June 6th, 1918, when the right flank of an English brigade, which had been heavily engaged, was threatened by the enemy's advance, the battalion in reserve, the 1/4th Battalion of the King's Shropshire Light Infantry, was ordered to deliver a counter-attack against an important position, from which the garrison had been driven. With magnificent dash and after heavy fighting the position was recovered, and with it the key to the whole line of defence, which made it possible to re-establish the line and maintain it intact."

INTRODUCTION

At that time the battalion was serving with the 19th (New Army) Division, south-west of Reims, when the enemy was making one of his greatest efforts.

There were occasions when Territorial battalions earned the praise of British Divisional, Corps and Army Commanders, while they were serving in Regular or New Army formations; but we have not yet adopted the system of giving honours to units, although there is much to be said for it.

The Mounted Brigades, Artillery, Medical and Technical branches of the Force do not come within the scope of these Notes, but no assessment of its value would be just which neglected to take their services into account.

It is generally recognised that the defeat of Turkey helped to bring the end of the War nearer; it is not generally known, or realised, that the Force under Sir Edmund Allenby, which between 31st October and 9th December, 1917, smashed the Turks and cleared southern Palestine from Gaza and Beersheba to Joppa and Jerusalem, was practically a Territorial Army; nearly five-sixths of the Infantry belonged to that Force, while the mounted men were chiefly Yeomanry and Colonials.

At a conference as to the reorganisation of the Force held on 1st April, 1919, when the Secretary of State for War met representatives of the County Associations, Mr. Churchill said: " I could not meet

x   THE TERRITORIAL DIVISIONS

this body representing the Territorial Associations of the United Kingdom without expressing on behalf of the War Office and on behalf of King and country our profound gratitude to the Territorial Force for the services which they have rendered in the Great War. There have been killed in the Territorial Force more than 6,500 officers, and more than 105,000 men; and in the killed, wounded, and missing, 26,900 officers and 565,000 men are included. This Force, which in so many quarters was hardly regarded seriously as a military factor before the Great War, has sent 1,045,000 men to fight against the best troops of Germany and of Turkey, and having sustained these terrible losses, has acquitted itself on all occasions in a manner which has won the whole-hearted acceptance of their Regular comrades and of the finest soldiers who have come to our assistance from the Dominions overseas. Twenty-nine officers and forty-two men of other ranks in the Territorial Force have gained the supreme honour of the Victoria Cross."

As some of the principal newspapers did not quote this part of Mr. Churchill's remarks it is excusable to repeat it here.

Most grateful acknowledgment is made of the permission granted by the Controller of His Majesty's Stationery Office to quote the extracts given from the published despatches as appearing in the *Gazette*, also, of that of Messrs. J. M. Dent and Sons, Limited, to refer to their edition of *Sir Douglas Haig's Despatches*, December 1915—April 1919, edited by Lieutenant-Colonel J. H. Boraston, O.B.E., Private Secretary to Earl Haig. Permission to refer to Sir Arthur Conan Doyle's *British Campaign in France and Flanders* has also very kindly been given. Although that work is not recognised as an official history, Sir Arthur had a very large mass of official material placed at his disposal, and much of the information he gives, particularly in regard to the work of divisions and the losses sustained by them in the big battles, is of great value. Thanks for similar permissions are also tendered to the author of *The Fifth Army in March* 1918, Mr. W. Shaw Sparrow, and his publishers Messrs. John Lane, The Bodley Head, Limited, and to the author of *The Story of the Fourth Army*, Major-General Sir Archibald Montgomery, K.C.M.G., C.B., and his publishers Messrs. Hodder and Stoughton, Limited. In a letter signifying his approval, Major-General Montgomery remarks: "I know what excellent work the Territorial Divisions did and I hope that they will always get full credit for it."

CONTENTS

	PAGE
INTRODUCTION	v
42ND (EAST LANCASHIRE) DIVISION. First Line	1
43RD (WESSEX DIVISION), First Line. 44TH (HOME COUNTIES DIVISION), First Line. 45TH (WESSEX) DIVISION, Second Line	15
46TH (NORTH MIDLAND) DIVISION. First Line	21
47TH (LONDON) DIVISION, FORMERLY 2ND LONDON. First Line	29
48TH (SOUTH MIDLAND) DIVISION. First Line	41
49TH (WEST RIDING) DIVISION. First Line	51
50TH (NORTHUMBRIAN) DIVISION. First Line	59
51ST (HIGHLAND) DIVISION. First Line	75
52ND (LOWLAND) DIVISION. First Line	91
53RD (WELSH) DIVISION. First Line	109
54TH (EAST ANGLIAN) DIVISION. First Line	121
55TH (WEST LANCASHIRE) DIVISION. First Line	129
56TH (LONDON) DIVISION, FORMERLY 1ST LONDON. First Line	141
57TH (WEST LANCASHIRE) DIVISION. Second Line	151
58TH (1ST LONDON) DIVISION. Second Line	155
59TH (NORTH MIDLAND) DIVISION. Second Line	165
60TH (2ND LONDON) DIVISION. Second Line	169
61ST (SOUTH MIDLAND) DIVISION. Second Line	179
62ND (WEST RIDING) DIVISION. Second Line	187
66TH (EAST LANCASHIRE) DIVISION. Second Line	195
APPENDIX	203

THE TERRITORIAL DIVISIONS

42ND (EAST LANCASHIRE) DIVISION
First Line

THE Division sailed for Egypt on September 10th, 1914, at a time when sanguine people thought that the only rôle of the Territorial Force would be to provide garrisons for our outlying Dependencies. It was the first Territorial division to leave Britain.

While in Egypt the Division supplied part of the Canal Defence Force, the Artillery and Engineers of the Division being engaged in February 1915, when the Turkish attack on the Canal was driven off. See despatches from Sir A. Wilson, C.B., dated 11th February, 1915, and 1st August, 1915. In the former, paragraph 37, the 19th Lancashire Battery R.F.A., T.F., was said to have rendered excellent service.

During the six months following their arrival in Egypt, the Division did much hard marching and training of all kinds.

At the beginning of May 1915 the Division embarked for the Dardanelles, and the Lancashire Fusilier Brigade, the 125th, disembarked on 5th May (see Sir Ian Hamilton's despatch of 20th May) in time to take part in the sanguinary fighting,

6th–10th May, now called the Second Battle of Krithia.

In his despatch of 26th August, 1915, Sir Ian Hamilton describes the struggle. Our tired troops had to attack formidable opposing lines, the enemy being well entrenched. The Brigade was attached temporarily to the 29th Division. A certain amount of progress was made on the 6th May. On the 7th at 3 p.m. the two brigades on the left, Lancashire Fusilier Brigade and 88th Brigade, were held up, but a general attack of the whole line ordered for 4.45 p.m. gained ground. Heavy counter-attacks were delivered till dawn on the 10th, these were repulsed. On the 11th the 42nd, which had completed its disembarkation on the 9th, relieved the 29th Division, now worn out after eighteen days' hard fighting. Shortly after this the Force settled down to what was practically siege warfare.

During the latter half of May the 42nd Division worked night and day on a series of new fire and communication trenches in " no man's land," which brought their front line within assaulting distance. On 25th May the Royal Naval and 42nd Divisions crept 100 yards nearer to the Turks, and on the night of May 28th/29th the whole British Line made a further small advance.

Each night till 3rd/4th June attacks by the enemy were made on the new line, but these were repulsed.

A general assault was ordered for the 4th June. This is now the Third Battle of Krithia. Sir Ian said: "The Manchester Brigade of the 42nd Division advanced magnificently. In five minutes the first line of Turkish trenches was captured and by

12.30 p.m. the Brigade had carried with a rush the line forming their second objective, having made an advance of 600 yards in all. The working parties got to work without incident and the position here could not possibly have been better."

Unfortunately the advance was not successful on the front of the 29th Division, on the left of the 42nd, while later there was a withdrawal of troops on the right. "The enfilade fire of the Turks began to fall upon the Manchester Brigade of the 42nd Division which was firmly consolidating the furthest distant line of trenches it had so brilliantly won. After 1.30 p.m. it became increasingly difficult for this gallant Brigade to hold its ground, heavy casualties occurred, the Brigadier and many other officers were wounded or killed, yet it continued to hold out with the greatest tenacity and grit. Every effort was made to sustain the Brigade in its position, its right flank was thrown back to make face against the enfilade fire. . . . It became clear that unless the right of our line could advance again it would be impossible for the Manchesters to maintain the very pronounced salient in which they now found themselves." Eventually "By 6.30 p.m. therefore the 42nd Division had to be extricated with loss from the second line Turkish trenches and had to content themselves with consolidating on the first line which they had captured within five minutes of commencing the attack. Such was the spirit displayed by this Brigade that there was great difficulty in persuading the men to fall back. Had their flanks been covered nothing would have made them loosen their grip. . . . About 400 prisoners were taken in the attack. The majority of these captures were made by the 42nd Division under Major-General W. Douglas."

The Division was not heavily engaged in the battles of 28th June and 12th-13th July.

The despatch of 11th December, 1915, contains an account of the Suvla Bay fighting and of certain operations undertaken on 6th-8th August at Helles to contain the enemy there. The 29th Division was to attack about 1200 yards of front and the 42nd was asked to capture two trenches. The Turks were found "full of fight." The 29th did not progress. "Two resolute separate attacks were made by the 42nd Division but both of these recoiled in face of the unexpected volume of fire developed by the Turks." The reason was that our attack and one by the Turks had almost coincided and the enemy trenches were full of men.

On August 7th the attack was renewed and there was again very heavy fighting. " In the centre a stiff battle raged all day up and down a vineyard. . . . A large portion of the vineyard had been captured in the first dash and the East Lancashire men in this part of the field stood their ground against a succession of vigorous counter-attacks. The enemy suffered very severely in these counter-attacks which were launched in strength and at short intervals. . . . Owing to the fine endurance of the 6th and 7th Battalions of the Lancashire Fusiliers it was found possible to hold the vineyard through the night, and a massive column of the enemy which strove to overwhelm their thinned ranks was shattered to pieces in the attempt. . . .

FORTY-SECOND DIVISION 5

For two more days the troops (42nd Division) were called upon to show their qualities of vigilance and power of determined resistance, for the enemy had by no means yet lost hope of wresting from us the ground we had won in the vineyard. This unceasing struggle was a supreme test for battalions already exhausted by 48 hours' desperate fighting, and weakened by the loss of so many good leaders and men, but the peculiar grit of the Lancastrians was equal to the strain, and they did not fail. Two specially furious counter-attacks were delivered by the Turks on the 8th August, one at 4.40 a.m., and another at 8.30 p.m., where again our bayonets were too much for them. Throughout the night they made continuous bomb attacks, but the 6th Lancashire Fusiliers and the 4th East Lancashire Regiment stuck gamely to their task at the eastern corner of the vineyard. There was desperate fighting also at the northern corner, where the personal bravery of Lieutenant W. T. Forshaw, 1/9th Manchester Regiment, who stuck to his post after his detachment had been relieved, an act for which he has since been awarded the V.C., was largely instrumental in the repulse of three very determined onslaughts."

By the morning of August 9th "things were quieter and the sorely tried troops were relieved." The fighting, 6th to 13th August, is now officially the "Actions of Krithia Vineyard."

The Division, which was now at little more than one-third of its establishment, received a reinforcement of dismounted yeomen in September. It was incidentally mentioned in Sir C. C. Monro's despatch of 6th March, 1916, regarding the evacuation of

6 THE TERRITORIAL DIVISIONS

Helles, as being, in December 1915, badly in need of rest. The losses of the Division on the Peninsula, killed, wounded and missing, the last being mostly killed, exceeded 8000.

After the evacuation, 8th January, 1916, the Division had a short stay at Mudros and was then taken to Egypt.

In Sir A. Murray's despatch of 1st October, 1916, dealing with operations east of the Canal, he stated that of the East Lancashire troops commanded by Major-General Sir W. Douglas, only two battalions were in action on the 4th August, now the Battle of Rumani, when the Turks were driven back with heavy loss, but he said that the force carried out a march under very trying conditions on the subsequent days.

At no time during their long war-service did the Division experience a greater physical strain than on this march. The 52nd on the left were nearer the coast, with its sea air, and on the whole had harder going. The two brigades of the 42nd were wading and struggling in loose desert sand while the heat was intense. Very many men collapsed. Sir A. Murray in the despatch, paragraph 5, said: "Vigorous action, to the utmost limits of endurance was ordered for the 5th August and the troops, in spite of the heat, responded nobly." Certainly the sufferings of the 127th Brigade on the 5th and 6th bounded on the limits of human endurance. The 125th had slightly better ground and a shorter distance. The 126th was in reserve.

The Division, along with the 52nd, alternately formed the advance guard, in co-operation with

FORTY-SECOND DIVISION 7

mounted troops, until the railhead reached El Arish, when it returned to Kantara. Before the end of February 1917 it had embarked at Alexandria for France.

After being re-equipped the Division as part of the III. Corps, Fourth Army, entered the line in the Epéhy district and thereafter held a sector about Havrincourt until 8th July, when they went out for rest and training in the back area of the Third Army, about the ground of the First Battle of the Somme.

In September 1917, the Division took over from the 15th in the Third Battle of Ypres, in the area of the Fifth Army. On 6th September they assaulted several fortified farms, but, in consequence of a little hill on the left being still in the enemy's possession, they failed to make much progress. Their losses were heavy, partly because the Division was so persistent in their pursuit of a success. During the following days they had further fighting.

On the 26th the Division relieved the 66th in the Coastal Sector at Nieuport. When relieved there by a French unit in November the 42nd moved to Givenchy. There they constructed many concrete defence works which earned the gratitude and praise of the 55th when the Lys battle opened on 9th April, 1918. See 55th Division.

When, early in 1918, brigades were reduced to three battalions, any surplus of men or of experience was transferred to the second line division, the 66th, a gift which was to be of inestimable value during the terrible fighting the 66th endured in the March Retreat.

8   THE TERRITORIAL DIVISIONS

About 23rd March, 1918, the 42nd were " bused " to the Arras—Bapaume area to assist in arresting the great German offensive. On the 24th they entered the line about Ervillers, and now had fighting of the most trying description ; the flanks being often " in the air," partly because divisions which had been in the battle since its commencement on the 21st were almost worn to the bone.

In a supplementary despatch of 23rd April, 1918, as to the work of different divisions, Sir Douglas Haig said: " In fierce fighting at end of March and early in April around Bucquoy and Ablainzevelle the 42nd (East Lancashire) Division (T.) and 62nd (West Riding) Division (T.) beat off many attacks and contributed greatly to the successful maintenance of our line in this important sector."

In Sir Douglas Haig's despatch of 20th July, 1918, as to the March Retreat, paragraph 33, Third Army front, he said: " A counter-attack by the 42nd Division, under Major-General A. Solly-Flood (on 25th March) drove the enemy out of Sapignies," and notwithstanding that the Germans maintained great pressure and made many attacks, the 42nd Division at end of the day held Ervillers " where the 1/10th Battalion Manchester Regiment, 42nd Division, had repulsed eight attacks." The fighting 24th/25th March is now the " First Battle of Bapaume, 1918." Paragraph 42, as to the 26th–27th March: " Elsewhere all his assaults were heavily repulsed by troops of the 62nd, 42nd and Guards Divisions."

Paragraph 45 deals with the great attack on 28th March, now officially the " First Battle of Arras,

FORTY-SECOND DIVISION 9

1918," when the fighting was "of the utmost intensity." " On the southern portion of his attack the enemy's repulse was, if possible, even more complete than on the new front east of Arras. . . . The 42nd Division drove off two attacks from the direction of Ablainzevelle."

The worst was over and the line now stabilised, but on the 5th and 6th April the enemy launched very heavy attacks in the neighbourhood where the 42nd were holding the line. See also 47th Division. These new attacks were also repulsed. This is now the " Battle of the Ancre, 1918."

In the *History of the 42nd Division* by Mr. F. P. Gibbon (*Country Life* Office, London, 1921, price 6s. 6d.) there is quoted an order by the Commander of the IV. Corps, Sir G. M. Harper, in which he said: " The Corps Commander congratulates 42nd Division on their magnificent behaviour during the last few days of fighting. Numerous heavy attacks have been made by the enemy and have been completely repulsed with heavy loss, and the capture of prisoners and machine-guns. He heartily thanks the troops for their courage and endurance, and is confident that they will continue to hold the line against all attacks."

The Divisional Commander also issued a special order congratulating the Division on their " magnificent work," and subsequently in his farewell order, dated 18th March, 1919, after referring to the Division being hurried in buses " to help in stemming the great enemy offensive," he said: " This it effectually did in an epic battle, in a manner which has earned for it undying fame. . . . For seventeen consecutive days it remained in action, and held its ground in a manner that cannot be surpassed by the performance of any troops in any period of history."

Mr. Gibbon states the losses of the Division between 24th March and 8th April at 2963. He makes it clear that on no occasion did the Division retire except under orders.

Throughout the summer the Division, with brief intervals, held the line about Gommecourt and Hebuterne, and when the Third Army attacked, on 21st August, the Division advanced through Serre.

The supplementary despatch of 13th September, 1918, said: " The 42nd Division, which, in the latter days of March, fought with great gallantry north of Bapaume, took part in the attack launched by us on the 21st August and in spite of obstinate resistance by the enemy captured Miraumont. During the following days it had heavy fighting on a number of occasions but, before the end of the month, reached and captured Riencourt-lez-Bapaume."

This good work was again referred to in the despatch of 21st December, 1918, paragraph 21 of which shows that at 4.55 a.m. on 21st August the IV. and V. Corps of the Third Army attacked, the 42nd Division being in the assaulting troops of the IV. Corps. " The enemy's foremost defences were carried rapidly and without difficulty."

The fighting 21st–23rd August is now officially designated the " Battle of Albert, 1918." Paragraph 22 deals with the fighting on 23rd and 24th August.

"Miraumont, which for three days had resisted our attacks, was taken by the 42nd Division (Major-General A. Solly-Flood) with many prisoners and, pressing forward, the same Division seized Pys."

Mr. Gibbon states that between 21st August and 6th September the Division took 1261 prisoners and 24 guns, and their casualties were 253 killed and 1305 wounded.

The fighting 31st August—3rd September is now the "Second Battle of Bapaume."

During the remainder of the "Advance to Victory," the 42nd alternated with the New Zealand Division in one of the two divisional sections of the IV. Corps.

On 27th September the Division attacked and broke through the portion of the old Hindenburg line between Havrincourt and Beaucamp. After two days' unceasing fighting they were able to claim over 1700 prisoners and nine field guns. Their own losses were about 1000.

In paragraph 35 of the despatch "The Battle of Cambrai and the Hindenburg line, 27th September—5th October," Sir Douglas Haig remarked: "The attack proceeded according to plan from the commencement. On the right strong resistance was encountered at Beaucamp. Several strong counter-attacks were made during the day in this neighbourhood, but in spite of them troops of the 5th and 42nd Divisions successfully established the right flank of our attack between Beaucamp and Ribecourt."

The fighting 27th September—1st October is now officially designated the "Battle of the Canal

12 THE TERRITORIAL DIVISIONS

du Nord," and that on 8th-9th October is the "Battle of Cambrai, 1918."

During the latter period the Division was resting about Havrincourt Wood but re-entered the line on the 12th.

On 20th October at 2 a.m. the Third Army and a portion of the First Army made an attack on the line of the Selle river, north of Le Cateau. On this occasion the Division carried all its four objectives. The despatch, paragraph 46, deals with the "Battle of the Selle," and states: "On this occasion also the enemy's resistance was serious, and he had been able to erect wire entanglements along the greater part of the line. Our advance was strongly contested at every point, frequent counter-attacks being made. Supported by a number of Tanks which had successfully crossed the river, our infantry after severe fighting . . . gained their objectives on the high ground east of the Selle, pushing out patrols as far as the river Harpies."

Paragraph 47 described another assault made on the 23rd October, in which the 42nd is included among the attacking troops. "At the end of the day the western outskirts of the Forêt de Mormal had been reached."

Both on the 20th and the 23rd there was much bitter and often hand-to-hand fighting. The 42nd had as its opponents a crack German division, fresh from reserve, the 25th and part of another, and success was only attained by a fine exhibition of skilful tactics and great fearlessness on the part of the troops. The Divisional R.E. did particularly well at the crossing of the Selle.

FORTY-SECOND DIVISION

The map opposite page 294 of Messrs. Dent's edition of *Sir Douglas Haig's Despatches* shows that the 42nd Division was among the troops employed at the Battle of the Sambre, commencing 4th November. The Division took over from the New Zealand Division in the Forêt de Mormal and, becoming the spear-head of the IV. Corps, kept up the pressure. This was a task of very great difficulty as the roads through the Forest had been mined and otherwise destroyed, and off the roads, owing to continued rain, the ground was a morass. In the words of a Special Order by the G.O.C. Division they "forced the passage of the bridgeless River Sambre in face of severe enemy fire and captured Hautmont."

On Armistice day the Division was just east of the Maubeuge—Avesnes road.

All through the "Advance to Victory" the work of the 42nd was up to the very high standard they themselves had set in Gallipoli in 1915, and unofficial writers have uniformly referred to their services in that Advance in terms of the highest praise.

In the Farewell Order before referred to Major-General Solly-Flood said: "From the 21st August until the Armistice on 11th November it played a continuous part in the great offensive. We can with reason be proud of the Division's share in that fighting. Its record includes an advance of 64 miles during which it fought in 12 general actions—each of several days' duration. Its captures include 18 towns and villages, over 4,000 prisoners, 37 guns of all calibre, 122 trench mortars, 455 machine guns and much other valuable booty.

14 THE TERRITORIAL DIVISIONS

"Early in 1918 I set the Division a motto: 'Go one better,' believing the spirit it expressed would always carry them to success. It has invariably acted up to that motto, and it is my pride to be able to say that never has the Division been called upon to undertake an operation in which it did not succeed, and never was it set a task which it did not more than accomplish."

These are the words of a friendly critic but they are something more than "faint praise." To have so thoroughly satisfied a Regular officer of the standing of their Commander meant service of great merit.

The foregoing account had been written and, like a number of those which follow, had been gone over by a senior officer of the Division before Mr. Gibbon's *History of the 42nd* was published, but the losses and certain other details concerning 1918 are as given by Mr. Gibbon. His chronicle gives a full account of the March battle and of the last Advance, and claims which he makes, such as that the losses of the Division were increased because it attained its objectives up to time and while its flanks were uncovered, are substantiated by other authorities.

43RD (WESSEX) DIVISION. FIRST LINE
44TH (HOME COUNTIES) DIVISION. FIRST LINE
45TH (WESSEX) DIVISION. SECOND LINE

THESE three divisions sailed for the East early in the war, chiefly in September 1914, and were among the first Territorial units to leave Britain. As regards being mentioned in despatches as divisional units they were unfortunate, no such references having been made, but their services to the Empire were, nevertheless, very great.

It has been suggested that if these three divisions had been sent to France when they went East, two months' intensive training would have fitted them to be of use in the First Battle of Ypres, certainly they might have been veterans before the Second. They would have stood the climatic conditions much better than the two Indian divisions, and a vast amount of shipping might have been saved. Probably political reasons demanded that a representation from India should appear on the Western Front, while, as Mr. Churchill said on 1st April, 1919, the Territorial Force was, in many quarters, hardly regarded seriously as a military factor before the Great War.

The public has learned that over 20,000 Territorials were still in India in the beginning of 1919 and were not relieved until the close of that year. Throughout the war, and for a year after the

16 THE TERRITORIAL DIVISIONS

Armistice, the garrison of India was largely composed of these divisions, but units of all three saw much heavy fighting in various theatres. It should be remembered also that facilities for leave did not exist in the East.

Doubtless imperious necessity compelled the breaking up of these divisions, and the sending of a battalion in one direction and its sister units in others.

In the despatches from India and Mesopotamia one misses that appreciation, so freely given by Sir John French to even individual battalions of the Territorial Force in the early stages of the war on the western front, and in these Eastern despatches the letters T.F. are not appended to the names of battalions. In Lists of Mention, however, this omission is remedied.

In Sir John Nixon's despatch of 1st January, 1916, thirty-five officers and men of the Hampshire Regiment, T.F., were mentioned for good services on the Euphrates, 26th June to 25th July, 1915.

About the close of 1915 and early in 1916 the 1/4th Hampshire Regiment, 1/4th Somersetshire Light Infantry and 1/4th Devonshire Regiment, all of the 43rd, and 1/5th Royal West Surrey and 1/5th East Kent Regiments of the 44th Division were in the Mesopotamia Army and had heavy casualties. Some of the 43rd Division were actually in Kut when it was besieged and were taken prisoners on the surrender of General Townshend's force. Other battalions of these three divisions sent drafts from India to Mesopotamia, which were, for the most part, attached to Regular regiments.

FORTY-THIRD DIVISION 17

Officers and other ranks of the 4th East Kent, 4th Devons, 6th Devons, and 2/5th Hampshire were mentioned in General Maude's last despatch.

In September 1918, the 1/4th Hampshire of the 43rd was serving in a force which was operating in Transcaspia.

There was published by the War Office on 13th January, 1920, a list of names, brought forward by Lieut.-General W. R. Marshall, K.C.B., for distinguished and gallant services with the Mesopotamia Expeditionary Force; the following units are represented in it:

43rd Division	1/4th and 1/6th Devonshire
	1/4th Somersetshire Light Infantry
	1/4th and 1/6th Hampshire
	1/4th Dorsetshire
44th Division	1/5th Royal West Surrey
	1/5th East Kent
	1/5th East Surrey
	1/5th Royal West Kent
	1/9th Middlesex
45th Division	2/7th Hampshire
	2/6th Devonshire

The 1/5th Duke of Cornwall's Light Infantry, originally of the 43rd, were Pioneers to the 61st Division in France in March 1918, and a successful counter-attack by the battalion is referred to in paragraph 31 of Sir Douglas Haig's despatch of 20th July, 1918.

The 1/7th and 1/8th Middlesex of the 44th served throughout most of the war with the 56th London

18 THE TERRITORIAL DIVISIONS

Division in France. The 1/7th was selected for the Army of the Rhine.

The 2/4th Royal West Surrey, the 2/10th Middlesex and the 2/4th Royal West Kent of the 67th, Second Line, Home Counties Division, served with the 53rd, Welsh, Division and saw much fighting at Suvla Bay, Gallipoli, and in Palestine. Latterly the 2/4th West Surrey was in France, and was selected for the Army of the Rhine.

Sir A. Wilson's despatch of 1st March, 1916, deals with operations in Western Egypt at the close of 1915, and the beginning of 1916. He mentions the 2/7th and 2/8th Middlesex, of the 67th Division, as forming part of the force employed.

When in April 1918 the 52nd Division and other troops were taken from Palestine to France certain units of these divisions were brought to Palestine and along with the Indian troops were engaged in the last victorious operations in that sphere. Among the mentions by Sir E. Allenby for good work in Palestine, March to September 1918, the following battalions are represented:

43rd Division	1/4th Duke of Cornwall's Light Infantry
	1/5th Somersetshire Light Infantry
	1/4th and 1/5th Devonshire Regiment
	1/4th Wiltshire Regiment
45th Division	2/5th Hampshire Regiment
	2/4th Dorset Regiment

The 1/5th Devonshire of the 43rd and the 2/4th

FORTY-THIRD DIVISION 19

Hampshire of the 45th joined the 62nd Division in France in June 1918 and were with it until the Armistice. When the 62nd was with the French Army on the Ardre, upon the east side of the salient between the Aisne and the Marne, in July 1918, these two battalions did work which was highly spoken of and quite worthy of the famous division to which they were attached. They gained a large number of awards in the last five months' fighting. This remark applies particularly to the 2/4th Hampshire, the number of whose awards for work in France was quite exceptional. As to the 62nd Division, see *The West Riding Territorials in the Great War*, Kegan Paul and Co. Both the above battalions were chosen for the Army of Occupation.

The official lists issued by the War Office in November 1920 showed that awards were gained by a non-commissioned officer of the 1/4th East Kent for valuable service when with the Baluchistan Force, and by men of the 1/4th and 1/7th Hampshire for gallant service when with the Waziristan Force as late as 25th May, 1919.

For the Armies of Occupation there were chosen: Mesopotamia, the 1/5th East Kent, 1/5th Royal West Kent and 1/5th East Surrey of the 44th, and the 1/4th Dorsetshire of the 43rd. For Persia the 1/4th Hampshire of the 43rd. For Egypt the 1/4th Wiltshire and 1/5th Somerset Light Infantry of the 43rd, while the 1/8th Hampshire was also selected for Egypt and the 1/9th (Cyclists) for Siberia.

Although they were never operating as divisions the units from Wessex and the Home Counties can at least count themselves as very " far travelled."

46TH (NORTH MIDLAND) DIVISION
First Line

This Division sailed for France in February 1915. One brigade was in reserve at the Battle of Neuve Chapelle, 10th–13th March, see paragraph 4 of the despatch from Sir John French, dated 5th April, 1915. In that despatch, paragraph 9, Sir John French said: " Several T.F. Battalions were engaged in the most critical moments of the fighting which occurred in the middle of March and they acquitted themselves with the utmost credit." He looked forward to the T.F. troops being employed as divisions and said: " These opinions are fully borne out by the results of the close inspection I have recently made of the North Midland Division under Major-General The Hon. Montague-Stuart-Wortley and the 2nd London Division (afterwards the 47th) under Major-General Barter."

This generous appreciation gave great encouragement not only to those of the Force in France, but to those who were then preparing themselves to go abroad, as well as to those who were working for the Territorial Force at home.

The Division spent the next six months in front of Neuve Église and in the Ypres salient, and at times had sharp fighting. It was involved in the first " Flammenwerfer " attack but stood its ground and repelled the enemy.

22 THE TERRITORIAL DIVISIONS

The 46th Division is mentioned in Sir John French's last despatch dated 31st July, 1916, as having on 13th October, 1915, taken part in an attack on the Hohenzollern Redoubt and Fosse 8, near Loos. The Division retook the redoubt, but as they could make no progress up the trenches to Fosse 8, and as the Redoubt was commanded from Fosse 8, they were pressed back to the west edge of the Redoubt where they made a defensive line.

See also an authorised account by the Press Association Correspondent written on 24th November, 1915, who was then able to stand on the part captured and look back over the glacis crossed by the Division, who had done all that the bravest could do.

The Division was, in December 1915, ordered to Egypt; two brigades had arrived there when the move was countermanded and, in February 1916, it was concentrated in the Arras district, where it took over a sector hitherto held by our French allies.

Sir Douglas Haig's despatch of 23rd December, 1916, which deals with the Somme battle, paragraph 8 (Dent's edition), shows that the 46th and 56th Divisions, VII. Corps, Third Army, made a subsidiary attack at Gommecourt on 1st July, 1916. " The subsidiary attack at Gommecourt also forced its way into the enemy's positions; but there met with such vigorous opposition that, as soon as it was considered that the attack had fulfilled its object, our troops were withdrawn."

The losses of both the 46th and 56th Divisions were very heavy. None of the other divisions

FORTY-SIXTH DIVISION 23

operating north of La Boisselle succeeded in consolidating the ground gained on 1st July. At that part of the line the enemy seems to have expected the attack and had made the most ample preparation to meet it. The efforts of these divisions, however, certainly contributed to the success of those further south.

In March 1917, when there were signs of a German retreat, the Division was about Bucquoy, as part of the II. Corps, and at times had sharp fighting and considerable losses. Thereafter they were taken to the north of Arras, where they were when the Battle of Arras opened on 9th April.

The despatch of 25th December, 1917, paragraph 36, Dent's edition, deals with " Minor Operations " in the Lens area and states: " Substantial progress was made in this area on the 5th and 19th June, and five days later North Midland troops (46th Division, Major-General W. Thwaites) captured an important position on the slopes of a small hill south-west of Lens, forcing the enemy to make a considerable withdrawal on both sides of the river." On 28th June an attack was made by the 46th Division and the 3rd and 4th Canadian Divisions on a front of two and a half miles astride the Souchez river. " All our objectives were gained," and 300 prisoners taken.

At that time the Division was in the I. Corps. Sir A. Conan Doyle states that when they were taken out on 2nd July, after ten weeks' continuous service in the line, none of the battalions were more than 300 strong. The tasks set to their neighbours, the Canadians, and to the 46th involved almost constant fighting, many strong positions being assaulted between the middle of April and the end of June.

The Division remained in the Lens—Givenchy area for many months. They were frequently engaged about Givenchy when the enemy made his great effort in that district in April 1918 (see 55th Division). They took part in the first advance eastward which began at the end of August. In September they were relieved and taken south where on the 19th they joined the IX. Corps, Fourth Army, and they remained in it till the battle of one hundred days was closed by the Armistice.

In Sir Douglas Haig's despatch of 21st December, 1918, paragraph 36, "The Hindenburg Line broken," 29th September, he said, "On the Fourth Army front the 46th Division (Major-General G. F. Boyd) greatly distinguished itself in the capture of Bellenglise. The village is situated in the angle of the Scheldt canal, which, after running in a southerly direction from Bellicourt, here bends sharply to the east towards the Le Tronquoy tunnel. Equipped with life-belts and carrying mats and rafts, the 46th Division stormed the western arm of the canal at Bellenglise and to the north of it, some crossing the canal on footbridges which the enemy was given no time to destroy, others dropping down the sheer sides of the canal wall, and having swum or waded to the far side, climbing up the farther wall to the German trench lines on the eastern bank. Having captured these trenches, the attacking troops swung to the right and took from flank and rear the German defences along the eastern arm of the canal, and on the high ground

FORTY-SIXTH DIVISION 25

south of the canal, capturing many prisoners and German batteries in action before the enemy had had time to realise the new direction of the attack. So thorough and complete was the organisation for this attack, and so gallantly, rapidly and well was it executed by the troops, that this one division took on this day over 4000 prisoners and 70 guns."

This feat of arms seems to be as fine as anything done in the whole course of the war.

The despatch as published in the *Gazette* speaks of the 32nd Division passing through the 46th and taking Lehaucourt and Magny La Fosse, but according to the history of the 46th[1] the 46th captured these villages which were within their objectives. The 32nd then passed through them at 5.30 p.m. and next day took Levergies. The error is corrected by a note on page 283 of Messrs. Dent's *Sir Douglas Haig's Despatches*.

A detailed account of the battle of 29th September is given by Major-General Sir Archibald Montgomery in his *Story of the Fourth Army* (Hodder and Stoughton). Towards the close of that account he says: "The success attending the operations of the IX. Corps was primarily due to the dash and determination with which the troops of the 46th Division pressed forward to their objective, and to the excellent leadership and initiative of the subordinate commanders. When their flanks were exposed, they exerted pressure where the enemy was weak and gave way, and only strengthened their flanks just sufficiently to safeguard them."

[1] *Breaking the Hindenburg Line. The Story of the 46th (North Midland) Division*, by Major Priestley. London. Fisher Unwin.

26 THE TERRITORIAL DIVISIONS

The fighting 29th September—2nd October is now designated the "Battle of St. Quentin Canal."

The Division captured Ramicourt and broke the Beaurevoir—Fonsomme line, after stiff fighting, on 3rd October—the "Battle of the Beaurevoir Line."

One brigade, the 139th, was attached to the 6th Division, for an attack on 8th October when Mannequin Hill and other strong positions were captured. (*Story of Fourth Army*, pp. 194 and 195.)

The Division was in the line on 9th and 10th October during the "Battle of Cambrai, 1918," when rapid progress was made until they were stopped at Riquerval Wood. They were again employed in the Battle of the Selle River, 17th–25th October, see paragraphs 37 and 46 of the despatch.

In his *Breaking the Hindenburg Line*, Major Priestley gives detailed accounts of the Battle of Ramicourt, 3rd October, and the Battle of Andigny or Riquerval, a phase of the Battle of the Selle, 17th and 18th October. He points out that on the 3rd, the 46th not only took Ramicourt but captured and cleared Montbrehain to the east of it, 1000 prisoners being taken in the latter place; but, in consequence of the Division on the left of the 46th having been held up, the latter had to withdraw from Montbrehain, establishing their line to the west of it. He also mentions that both on the 3rd and 17th/18th October, as well as in the preliminary actions between these dates, the enemy's resistance was much more stubborn than at Bellenglise, where the crossing of the canal had probably upset all his calculations and temporarily knocked the heart out of him.

FORTY-SIXTH DIVISION 27

The IX. Corps took part in the "Battle of the Sambre," 4th November, and continued to move forward till the 10th November. The 46th Division, which had been out at rest from 18th October till 1st November, on the night of the 4th relieved brigades of the 1st and 32nd Divisions and continued to press and pursue the enemy. On the evening of the 6th they entered Cartignies and on the 7th, in face of resistance, crossed the Petite Helpe. On the 8th they had crossed the La Capelle—Avesnes road and when the Armistice came the Division was east of Sains.

The 1/5th South Staffordshire was selected for the Army of the Rhine.

47TH (LONDON) DIVISION, FORMERLY 2ND LONDON. FIRST LINE

THE 47th Division went to France in March 1915, and a reference to its being inspected by Sir John French will be found under the 46th. In his despatch of 15th June, 1915, Sir John French mentioned that the First Army made an effort to advance its line in the Neuve Chapelle—Festubert district during May, the Battle of Festubert, and said, paragraph 5: " On 24th and 25th May the 47th Division (2nd London Territorial) succeeded in taking some more of the enemy's trenches, and in making good the ground gained to the east and north." Various writers say that in this, the Division's first big battle, they made a very fine advance and held the ground gained against many counter-attacks, during the succeeding days.

In Sir John French's despatch of 15th October, 1915, as to the Battle of Loos, etc., he said that the 47th Division was on the extreme right of the British Army on 25th September. Paragraph 10: " The 47th Division on the right of the IV. Corps rapidly swung its left forward and occupied the southern outskirts of Loos and a big double slag-heap opposite Grenay known as the Double Crassier. Thence it pushed on and by taking possession of the cemetery, the enclosures and chalk pits south of Loos, succeeded

30 THE TERRITORIAL DIVISIONS

in forming a strong defensive flank. The London Territorial Division acquitted itself most creditably. It was skilfully led and the troops carried out their task with great energy and determination. They contributed largely to our success in this part of the field."

Paragraph 11: "As the success of the 47th Division on the right of the IV. Corps caused me less apprehension of a gap in our line near that point I ordered the Guards Division up to Nœux-les-Mines."

Paragraph 15, 27th September: "The 47th Division on the right of the Guards captured a wood further to the south and repulsed a severe hostile counter-attack"; and later: "The Division made a little more ground to the south, capturing one field gun and a few machine guns."

Sir Douglas Haig's despatch of 19th May, 1916, Messrs. Dent's edition, paragraph 3, shows that the 47th (Major-General Sir C. St. L. Barter) and 25th Divisions were holding positions on the Vimy Ridge on 21st May, 1916, when the enemy attacked, making "a small gain of no strategic or tactical importance."

The Division was taken to the Somme, and the despatch of 23rd December, 1916, paragraph 27 (Dent's edition), shows that as part of the III. Corps, Fourth Army, it was in the attack of 15th September, 1916. "On our left High Wood was at last carried, after many hours of very severe fighting, reflecting great credit on the attacking battalions of the 47th Division."

Paragraph 31, note, shows the Division was employed on 1st October, 1916, in a successful attack

FORTY-SEVENTH DIVISION 31

on Eaucourt l'Abbaye and the defences east and west of it.

A week later the Division made an attack on the Butte de Warlencourt, an extremely strong point, but were not successful. Already the mud was making movement almost impossible. The fighting 15th–22nd September is now designated the Battle of Flers-Courcelette, and that between 1st and 18th October the "Battle of the Transloy Ridges."

The despatch of 25th December, 1917, paragraph 33 (Dent's edition), contains an account of the Messines battle on 7th June, 1917. "Heavy fighting took place in Wytschaete and further north. London troops (47th Division, Major-General Sir G. F. Gorringe) encountered a serious obstacle in another strong point known as the White Château. This redoubt was captured while the morning was yet young." The 41st and 47th had further resistance in Ravine Wood, "killing many Germans." In this battle the 47th Division was in the X. Corps, Second Army.

The 47th Division was in the later stages of the Third Battle of Ypres in the autumn of 1917, see *History of the 25th Division*, by Col. Kincaid-Smith, Harrison and Sons, page 94. They were in the undesirable Glencorse Wood area. About the third week of August they relieved the 8th Division, and as part of the II. Corps had heavy fighting about 22nd to 24th August when, at serious cost, their line was advanced. On 9th September they took over from the 25th in the same district.

In Sir Douglas Haig's despatch of 20th February, 1918, dealing with the "Battle of Cambrai, 1917," he said, paragraph 11, German attack of 30th November, 1917: " In the northern area the German attack was not launched until some two hours later. This was the enemy's main attack and was carried out with large forces and great resolution.

" After a preliminary bombardment and covered by an artillery barrage the enemy's infantry advanced shortly after 9 a.m. in dense waves, in the manner of his attack in the first battle of Ypres. In the course of the morning and afternoon no less than five principal attacks were made in this area, and on one portion of the attack as many as eleven waves of German infantry advanced successively to the assault. On the whole of this front a resolute endeavour was made to break down by sheer weight of numbers the defence of the London Territorials and other English battalions holding the sector."

" In this fighting the 47th (London) Division, T." (Major-General Sir G. F. Gorringe) (which had entered the battle on the night of the 28th–29th November), " the 2nd Division and the 56th (London) Division, T., greatly distinguished themselves and there were accomplished many deeds of great heroism." After describing attacks made during the day, which were driven back, the enemy's losses being enormous, the despatch says: " Early in the afternoon the enemy again forced his way into our foremost positions in this locality (west of Bourlon), opening a gap between the 1/6th and 1/15th Battalions, London Regiment. Counter-attacks led by the two battalion commanders with all available men, including the personnel of their headquarters, once more restored the situation. All other attacks were beaten off with the heaviest losses to the enemy.

"The greatest credit is due to the troops at Masnières (29th Division), Bourlon and Mœuvres for the very gallant service performed by them on this day. But for their steady courage and staunchness in defence the success gained by the enemy on the right of our battle front might have had serious consequences."

Paragraph 13, withdrawal from Bourlon, etc., night of 4th/5th December, 1917: "Much skill and courage were shown by our covering troops in this withdrawal, and an incident which occurred on the afternoon of 6th December, in the neighbourhood of Graincourt, deserves special notice. A covering party, consisting of two companies of the 1/15th Battalion London Regiment, 47th Division, much reduced in strength by the fighting at Bourlon Wood, found their flank exposed by a hostile attack further east and were enveloped and practically cut off. These companies successfully cut their way through to our advanced line of resistance, where they arrived in good order after having inflicted serious casualties on the enemy." As to the Cambrai battle see also under 51st, 55th, 56th and 62nd Divisions.

The Division was moved south, and in January 1918 took over in the Ribecourt area of the Flesquières salient, east of Havrincourt Wood. As part of the V. Corps, Third Army, it was involved in the March Retreat although perhaps not so seriously as the Fifth Army further south. In his despatch of

20th July, 1918, paragraph 17, speaking of the events of 21st March, Sir Douglas Haig said: "The enemy's advance south and north of the Flesquières salient rendered a withdrawal by the V. Corps and by the 9th Division on its right necessary also." Orders were issued accordingly. These different withdrawals were carried out successfully during the night. Paragraph 21: "The Divisions holding the Flesquières salient were not seriously involved during the morning of 22nd March but in the evening strong attacks were made both at Villers Plouich and at Havrincourt. All these attacks were repulsed with great slaughter."

Paragraph 28, 23rd March: "At the junction of the Third and Fifth Armies the situation was less satisfactory and as the day wore on it became critical."

As the result of the withdrawal of the VII. Corps, Fifth Army, a gap was formed between the flanks of the V. and VII. Corps though " vigorous efforts were made " by the 47th Division of the V. Corps and the 2nd of the VII. Corps to establish touch. These were unsuccessful; consequently, " The right of the V. Corps was forced back by pressure from the south-east first to Four Winds Farm, south of Ytres, where troops of the 47th Division made a gallant stand until nightfall."

Paragraph 30, as to 24th March: "The 47th Division held the village of Rocquiny from sunrise until well into the afternoon, beating off all attacks with rifle and machine-gun fire until the enemy worked round their flank and forced them to withdraw."

FORTY-SEVENTH DIVISION 35

On the 25th the Division, now very exhausted, was again heavily attacked near Contalmaison but successfully repulsed the enemy. The retreat was continued across the Ancre to about Bouzincourt north of Albert and, with intervals of rest, the Division remained in that area till the British advanced in August, although not always exactly in the same portion of the line.

The fighting 21st-23rd March is now designated the " Battle of St. Quentin," and that on the 24th-25th the " First Battle of Bapaume."

The Division was engaged near Albert when the enemy attacked the four British Divisions in that neighbourhood, 4th, 5th, and 6th April, the " Battle of the Ancre, 1918." The attack was pressed by large forces with great vigour and determination, but the line, though dented, remained unbroken. The depleted and weary ranks of the 47th responded to every call.

In his *Fifth Army in March* 1918 (John Lane, 1921), perhaps the most searching, fearless, and able work published in Britain on the war on land, Mr. Sparrow comments on those passages of the despatch which deal with the withdrawal from the Flesquières salient and the subsequent loss of connection between the Third and Fifth Armies. Mr. Sparrow thinks that the gap was caused primarily by the delay on the part of the V. Corps in withdrawing from the salient, and secondly because that corps, of which the 47th was the right division, tended north from the boundary line previously laid down by G.H.Q. He shows that the VII. Corps of the Fifth Army, although hardly pressed, did its best to maintain connection, and with that object crossed the boundary into Third Army ground. He concludes that the northward trend of the V. Corps was partly attributable to the break in the Third Army front about Lagnicourt. Doubtless this was the case. Certainly the Third Army was in very serious difficulties between the 21st and 29th, and its withdrawals were sometimes more rapid and carried further than those of the Fifth. To assume that all the " breaks " were on the front of the Fifth is to ignore the despatch itself.

In his telegraphic despatch of 13th September, 1918, as to the work of various divisions, Sir Douglas Haig said: " The 47th was continuously engaged in March throughout the retreat, fighting successful rearguard actions from La Vacquerie to Albert. Going into line on August 13th, in the neighbourhood of Morlancourt, it fought its way forward to St. Pierre-Vaast Wood, which it cleared of the enemy, overcoming fierce hostile resistance and capturing many prisoners and several guns in the course of its advance. Included among the latter was a German field gun battery which was rushed while in action firing over open sights."

The Division was then in the III. Corps, Fourth Army.

The despatch of 21st December, 1918, paragraph 21, shows that the III. Corps including the 47th, 12th and 18th Divisions attacked on 22nd August, during the " Battle of Albert, 1918 "; the 3rd Australian and 38th Divisions co-operated. The left

FORTY-SEVENTH DIVISION 37

of the Fourth Army was brought forward and over 2400 prisoners and a few guns were taken.

Paragraph 22. The III. Corps again attacked on the 23rd and progress was made. At 1 a.m. on the 24th the latter was renewed, the 3rd Australian Division took Bray-sur-Somme and the 47th, 12th, and 18th Divisions carried the line across the high ground between Bray and La Boisselle and took prisoners.

Paragraph 24. In support of the operation against Mont St. Quentin " on the morning of 31st August the left of the Fourth Army (3rd Australian Division, 58th London, 47th and 18th) attacked towards Bouchavesnes, Rancourt and Fregicourt, and by successful fighting on this and the following day, captured these villages and several hundred prisoners." The fighting 31st August—3rd September is now the " Second Battle of Bapaume." See also under 58th Division.

In the *History of the Fourth Army* (Hodder and Stoughton) there will be found an account which correlates the doings of the III. Corps and the Australian Corps in the fighting between 22nd August and 4th September. On several occasions the task of the 47th Division was a very hard one as at the " Happy Valley " on 22nd August and subsequently. At page 111 there occurs the following sentence: " The operations of the III. Corps were also worthy of the highest praise. The advance of this Corps from the capture of Albert on August 22nd, until they crossed the Canal du Nord on September 4th, covers a distance, as the crow flies, of some fourteen miles, over the desolate, shell-pitted area of the old Somme battlefields. The operations require to be studied in greater detail than is possible here before the magnitude of the task the troops were asked to perform, and the demands on the officers and men which such an advance in face of determined opposition entailed, can be fully realised. The spirit, however, of the young soldiers of the 12th, 18th, 47th and 58th Divisions successfully overcame every difficulty, and well did they answer every call made on them, and uphold the best traditions of the British soldier by their cheerfulness and endurance."

The Division left the III. Corps on 7th September and moved north to join the Fifth Army, and it was not thereafter in any hard-fought battle. Shortly thereafter Headquarters of the III. Corps also moved north to the Flanders area, where they were employed during the closing weeks.

For a time the 47th was in the line in the Lys area and after a short rest moved through Armentières to Lille, and, continuing to press and follow up the enemy, the Division was east of Tournai when the Armistice was concluded.

At Loos, in September 1915, the 47th Division had earned and received the praise of the Commander-in-Chief, Sir John French. In the next big battle—the Somme—at High Wood, September 1916, it had fought so well as again to be commended by the then Commander-in-Chief, Sir Douglas Haig, and at Bourlon Wood on 30th November, 1917, it " greatly distinguished " itself. Few if any divisions in the British Army received such recognition on three separate occasions. This most brilliant

FORTY-SEVENTH DIVISION 39

reputation remained, as will be seen from the foregoing extracts, absolutely untarnished to the end.

The 1/6th London Regiment, originally belonging to the 56th, but which served with the 47th Division, was selected for the Army of the Rhine.

NOTE.—In *Happy Days with the 47th and 49th Divisions*, by Benedict Williams (Harding and More, 1921, 7s. 6d.), there will be found many graphic descriptions of scenes in the Great Retreat, in the Advance from Albert in August and September, and in the final movements through Lille and Tournai.

48TH (SOUTH MIDLAND) DIVISION
FIRST LINE

THE 48th Division sailed for France in March 1915. The outstanding features in their war experiences are their long and memorable services in the Battle of the Somme in 1916, and in the Third Battle of Ypres, 1917, and their most successful advance in Italy in the last few days of the war with Austria.

The Division was present as part of the VIII. Corps at the Somme on 1st July, when the battle commenced, but fortunately for them they were in support that day and had an opportunity of learning from the misfortunes of the divisions in the front rank at that part of the line. The fighting 1st–13th July is now designated the " Battle of Albert, 1916." About 15th July the Division was transferred to the III. Corps.

On 16th July the 143rd Brigade made a very fine advance in the " Battle of Bazentin Ridge," and the capture of Ovillers was completed, the Division securing ground to the north and east of the village. During the ensuing fortnight the Division had constant and very heavy fighting.

Pozières was the next objective. The Australians attacked from the south on 23rd July and the 48th on their left from the south-west. Both attacks were pushed home with splendid resolution and by the 29th July the 48th had secured its objectives north of the village. On the 27th the 145th Brigade did exceptionally well. After a short rest the Division was, about 10th August, again in the line, pushing towards the ridge. A strong counter-attack was driven back on the 17th and on the 18th the 143rd Brigade captured a big stretch of trenches and 600 prisoners. The fighting 23rd July–3rd September is now designated the "Battle of Pozières Ridge." There were few tougher struggles in the whole course of the war.

When the arrival of winter and oceans of mud made offensive operations an impossibility, the Division, as part of the III. Corps, was still on the Somme.

In the despatch of 23rd December, 1916, paragraph 14 (Dent's edition), Sir Douglas Haig said: "On the 16th July a large body of the garrison of Ovillers surrendered, and that night and during the following day, by a direct advance from the west across No Man's Land, our troops (48th Division, Major-General R. Fanshawe) carried the remainder of the village and pushed out along the spur to the north and eastwards towards Pozières."

Paragraph 17: "An assault delivered simultaneously on this date—23rd July—by General Gough's Army (1st Australian Division and 48th Division) against Pozières gained considerable results, and by the morning of 25th July the whole of that village was carried, including the cemetery, and important progress was made along the enemy's trenches to the north-east."

Paragraph 19: "Apart from the operations already described others of a minor character, yet involving

FORTY-EIGHTH DIVISION 43

much fierce and obstinate fighting, continued during this period (August). Our lines were pushed forward," etc. Among the troops mentioned in a note as engaged was the 48th Division.

In February 1917 the enemy opposite Gough's Fifth Army commenced to withdraw, and early in March the Fourth Army found a similar movement commencing on their front. The 48th were then in the Fourth Army.

The despatch of 31st May, 1917, as to the German Retreat, paragraph 13 (Dent's edition), states: "At 7 a.m on the 18th March our troops (48th Division, Major-General R. Fanshawe) entered Peronne and occupied Mont St. Quentin, north of the town." Paragraph 16 shows that the Division "after fighting of some importance" on 4th and 5th April took part in the capture of Ronssoy and other villages. At this time the Division formed part of the XV. Corps, Fourth Army. In the *History of the Fourth Army* by Major-General Sir A. Montgomery (Hodder and Stoughton) at page 93, the Advance to Peronne, on 29th August, 1918, there is a note which says that the whole ground was familiar to the Fourth Army as they had crossed it in the early spring of 1917. "The first troops to reach the eastern bank on that occasion had been those of the 48th Division. They had secured Biaches and La Maisonette and then, forcing a crossing where the embankment of the Canal du Nord crossed the Somme south-west of Halle, had seized Mont St. Quentin."

The despatch of 25th December, 1917, Third Battle of Ypres, as to the attack on the 16th August (Dent's edition), states, paragraph 46: "On the left

44 THE TERRITORIAL DIVISIONS

centre West Lancashire Territorials and troops from other English Counties (48th and 11th Divisions) established themselves on a line running north from St. Julien to the old German third line due east of Langemarck. This line they maintained against the enemy's attacks and thereby secured the flank of our gains further north." Officially this is the Battle of Langemarck, 1917.

Paragraph 54, as to the attack on 4th October: "On the left of our attack South Midland troops (48th Division) forced their way across the valley of the Stroombeek, in spite of difficulties due to the rain of the previous night, and gained their objectives according to programme, with the exception of a single strong point at the limit of their advance." Officially this is now the Battle of Broodseinde.

Paragraph 56, as to the attack on 9th October: "Australian troops, East Lancashire, Yorkshire and South Midland Territorials (66th, 49th and 48th Divisions) carried our line forward in the direction of Passchendaele and up the western slopes of the main ridge capturing Nieuwemolen," etc. Officially this attack is now the Battle of Poelcappelle.

During these operations the Division was in the XVIII. Corps. No division had a longer spell of the great struggle known as the Third Battle of Ypres, and to say that any did better would be making a bold claim. They were in support on the opening day, 31st July, and apart from the actions mentioned in the above extracts, they made successful advances on 19th, 22nd and 27th August and had heavy fighting on many other days, while they endured very great hardships for nearly three months.

Before the close of 1917, the Division, along with other troops, was taken to Italy to assist in arresting the Austrian invasion. In the Earl of Cavan's despatch of 14th September, 1918, as to the operations of the British Army in Italy, he said: " Early in the morning of June 15th, after a short but violent bombardment, in which smoke and gas were freely employed, the Austrian attack was launched. The fronts of attack extended from St. Dona di Piave to the Montello on the plains and from Grappa to Canove in the mountains, fronts of 25 miles and 18 miles respectively. The whole of the British sector was involved.

" The British front was attacked by four Austrian divisions. It was held by the 23rd Division on the right and the 48th Division on the left. On the front of the 23rd Division the attack was completely repulsed. On the front of the 48th Division the enemy succeeded in occupying our front trench for a length of some 3000 yards and subsequently penetrated to a depth of 1000 yards. Here he was contained by a series of switches which had been constructed to meet this eventuality. On the morning of June 16th the 48th Division launched a counter-attack to clear the enemy from the pocket he had gained. This attack was completely successful and the entire line was re-established by 9 a.m.

" Acting with great vigour on the 16th both divisions took advantage of the disorder in the enemy's ranks and temporarily occupied certain posts in the Asiago plateau without much opposition. Several hundred prisoners and many machine guns and two mountain howitzers were brought back in broad daylight without interference. As soon as No Man's Land had been fully cleared of the enemy we withdrew to our original line. The enemy suffered very heavy losses in their unsuccessful attack. In addition we captured 1060 prisoners, seven mountain guns, 72 machine guns, 20 flammenwerfer and one trench mortar."

In a telegram of 3rd November Lord Cavan mentioned that the 48th Division was advancing on the Asiago plateau and had taken 100 guns.

In his despatch of 15th November, 1918, as to the concluding operations on the Italian front, Lord Cavan stated, paragraph 30, that the 48th Division, Major-General Sir H. B. Walker, K.C.B., D.S.O., had been employed on the Asiago plateau as part of the 6th Italian Army. It formed part of the XII. Italian Corps. "Successful raids were carried out on the 4th, 11th and 23rd October, which resulted in the capture of 445 prisoners and 12 machine guns."

Raids and patrols on 29th and 30th October found that the enemy were moving back, and a general advance of the 6th Italian Army was ordered. The 48th British and a French Division were the first to move. On 1st November the 4th Royal Berkshire Regiment captured Mont Catz.

"On the morning of 2nd November the success gained on Mont Catz by the 145th Infantry Brigade was widely exploited. Mont Mosciagh was in the hands of the 48th Division by 7.30 a.m. and the Interrotto position was thus outflanked. The advance then became more rapid, and by dark the

FORTY-EIGHTH DIVISION 47

advanced guards had reached Vezzena, and thus set foot on Austrian soil. This Division was therefore the first British division to enter enemy territory on the western front." The 4th Berkshire was part of the 145th Brigade.

"On the morning of 3rd November the advance was again resumed and by dark both Caldonazzo and Levico had been occupied.

"At 3 p.m. on 4th November when the Armistice (with Austria) came into force, the leading troops were on the line Miola—eastern outskirts of Trent.

"The captures in prisoners and guns made by the 48th Division cannot be accurately ascertained: they amounted to at least 20,000 prisoners and 500 guns. Included amongst the prisoners were the Commander of the III. Corps and three Divisional Commanders.

"It must be remembered that this division was attacking very formidable mountain positions with only a fifth part of the artillery that would have been at its disposal had the initial attack started on the Altipiano. Its performance therefore in driving in the enemy's rearguards so resolutely while climbing up to heights of 5000 feet, is all the more praiseworthy.

"During these operations the leadership of Brigadier-General G. C. Sladen, C.M.G., D.S.O., M.C., commanding the 143rd Infantry Brigade, was particularly noticeable.

"31. The infantry had been waiting for an opportunity to show that they could worthily emulate the performances of their comrades in

48 THE TERRITORIAL DIVISIONS

France. When the opportunity came they fulfilled my highest anticipations."

Lord Cavan's despatch of 15th November, 1918, paragraph 2, shows that three battalions of the 48th Division were taken to France on 13th/14th September of that year. These were the 1/8th Royal Warwickshire Regiment, 1/5th Gloucestershire Regiment, and 1/8th Worcestershire Regiment. They formed the reconstituted 75th Brigade in the 25th Division, which, after being sadly battered in the March Retreat, the Lys Battle of April and the German offensive on the Aisne at the end of May, had been withdrawn from the line and formed anew. The Division was concentrated in front of Combles on 3rd October and on the 4th commenced a hard struggle for the capture of Beaurevoir. This was completed by the 75th Brigade on the 5th after two previous attempts had failed. Sir A. Conan Doyle, vol. vi. p. 174, speaking of this achievement, says: " Fryell's 75th Brigade was now assembled in the dead ground west of Beaurevoir, and at about 6.30 dashed at it with levelled bayonets and a determination which would take no denial. The enemy were swept out of it and the line carried forward 500 yards to the east of it." Another account of the operation will be found at pp. 187 and 188 of *The Story of the Fourth Army*, and it is there remarked: " Perhaps the outstanding feature of the operations was the daylight attack of the 1/5th Gloucestershire and the 1/8th Worcestershire, which finally captured Beaurevoir village." At p. 198 of that work it is stated that the same brigade and a brigade of the 66th captured Maretz

FORTY-EIGHTH DIVISION 49

on the 9th. At p. 227 there is an account of a battle on 18th October when the 75th Brigade, which was temporarily attached to the 50th Division, again got credit by its capture of La Roux Farm and Bazuel and some heavy guns. P. 234 shows that the Brigade did fine work on the 23rd when the 1/8th Worcestershire captured Tilleuls Farm and a battery of howitzers.

On 4th November, the day on which the last battle of the war commenced, the Brigade gained great distinction by its capture of Landrecies, which involved the crossing of an unfordable canal. A detailed account will be found at p. 252 of *The Story of the Fourth Army*, and, regarding it, Major-General Montgomery says: "The capture of Landrecies was an operation beset with many difficulties, but, thanks to good leadership, the bravery of the troops, and the skill and devotion of the divisional engineers and pioneers, the 75th Brigade met with the success and good fortune which such a well planned and boldly executed operation deserved."

The History of the 25th Division (Harrison) also gives details of the splendid work of the 75th Brigade between 5th October and the close. See also the despatch of 21st December, 1918, paragraphs 37, 42, 47 and 50.

It is rather remarkable that in the short space of five weeks two men of the Brigade won the Victoria Cross.

The 1/7th Royal Warwickshire Regiment and 1/6th Gloucestershire Regiment were selected for the Army of Occupation, Egypt.

49TH (WEST RIDING) DIVISION

First Line

THE Division sailed for France in April 1915, and before the end of that month entered the line about Fleurbaix as part of the IV. Corps, First Army.

In the Battle of Aubers Ridge, 9th and other days of May 1915, the Division held most of the Corps line while the 7th and 8th Divisions attacked.

About the end of June the Division was transferred to the VI. Corps, Second Army, and thereafter did six months' arduous work in the Ypres salient.

In January 1916 the Division marched to Calais, whence, in February, they were railed to near Amiens. During the ensuing five months they held trenches in the Authuille—Thiepval district and did much work in preparation for the great battle. They were now in the Fifth Army, at first in the X. Corps, afterwards in the II.

From 1st July, 1916, when the Battle of the Somme opened, to nearly the end of September, they were almost constantly engaged, the task of the Fifth Army being to maintain vigorous pressure, and so facilitate the advance of the Fourth Army on its right. On the Division leaving the Fifth Army the Corps Commander expressed himself as gratified by their spirit and work.

The despatch from Sir Douglas Haig of 23rd December, 1916, paragraph 8, deals with the attack on Thiepval and other strongly fortified positions on 1st July, a phase of the "Battle of Albert, 1916," and in Messrs. Dent's edition, p. 26, there is a note in the following terms: "In the course of this fighting a brigade of the 49th Division, Major-General E. M. Percival, made a gallant attempt to force Thiepval from the north." The Division or one or other of the brigades was engaged in several subsequent actions in the Somme campaign of 1916.

The Division was taken north again in October to the Ypres area where it was to be employed for nearly two years. In July 1917 the Division moved from the Merville district to Nieuport where they experienced a particularly bad month. The hostile bombardment was ceaseless, and the troops in the line crowded in a very circumscribed space north of the Canal suffered very heavily. In the beginning of October the Division entered the main battle in the Ypres salient and took part in several attacks under most trying conditions; these were characteristic of the Third Battle of Ypres. A quotation as to the attack of 9th October, the Battle of Poelcappelle, has already been given under the 48th Division, who were on the left of the 49th, the 66th being on their right.

In November the Division was in the line in the Menin Road area, and although the great battle had died down losses from the unceasing shell fire kept high, while the physical sufferings from mud and cold were almost beyond the endurance of the strongest.

In January 1918, when brigades were cut down from four to three battalions, the 1/8th West York-

FORTY-NINTH DIVISION 53

shire Regiment, 1/5th West Riding Regiment and the 1/5th The King's Own Yorkshire Light Infantry were taken from the 49th and sent to the 62nd, the second line West Riding Division.

The 49th was still in the Ypres salient in the beginning of April 1918. Few divisions had a more intimate acquaintance with its shell-fire and mud.

The Division gained great distinction in the battles about the Lys river in April when the British were "fighting with their backs to the wall."[1] From 10th April till the end of that month one or other of the three brigades was almost daily engaged, on the northern side of the salient, which the enemy had made after overwhelming the Portuguese division on the 9th. The task of the 49th and other divisions near them was to stem his rush and prevent him spreading out to the north and west. If he had succeeded in gaining more ground to the north, Ypres would have gone.

In his written despatch of 20th July, 1918, as to these events Sir Douglas Haig said, paragraph 59, 12th April: "Troops of the 25th, 34th and 49th Divisions although heavily attacked maintained their positions to south and south-east of Bailleul."

Paragraph 60, 13th April: German troops had entered Neuve Église, "but before noon were driven out by troops of the 33rd and 49th Divisions in a most successful counter-attack in which a number of prisoners were taken."

Paragraph 64: "At different times on the 16th

[1] As to the Lys battles see also 50th, 51st, 55th and 61st Divisions.

54 THE TERRITORIAL DIVISIONS

April a number of strong local attacks were made by the enemy on the Meteren—Wytschaete front, which were for the most part repulsed with heavy loss by the 25th, 34th and 49th Divisions. . . . The enemy's attacks in the Kemmel sector (17th April) were pressed with great determination, but ended in his complete repulse at all points by troops of the 34th, 49th and 19th Divisions, his infantry being driven out by counter-attacks wherever they had gained a temporary footing in our line."

Paragraph 67 describes the fierce fighting on 25th and 26th April when the enemy captured Kemmel Hill. Speaking of the 25th, Sir Douglas Haig said the enemy's attacks were renewed in great strength, and after a violent bombardment. " The weight of the attack in the British sector fell on the 9th Division and attached troops of the 49th Division, who at 7 a.m. were still holding their positions about Wytschaete intact, though heavily engaged. Fierce fighting continued in this neighbourhood for some hours later, and great numbers of Germans were killed by rifle and machine-gun fire at short range. Later in the morning the right of the 9th Division was forced to fall back fighting stubbornly to Vierstraat, but at 1 p.m. our troops still held the Grand Bois north of Wytschaete."

The 49th was heavily engaged on the 26th. " A very gallant counter-attack by the 25th Division with attached troops of the 21st and 49th Divisions, undertaken in conjunction with the French, penetrated into Kemmel village, taking over 300 prisoners. Our troops then found themselves exposed to heavy machine-gun fire from the flanks

FORTY-NINTH DIVISION

and were unable to maintain their positions. Later in the morning the enemy renewed his attacks in strength but in spite of repeated efforts was only able to make small progress at certain points. Troops of the 21st, 30th, 39th and 49th Divisions and the South African Brigade of the 9th Division had heavy fighting and made several gallant counter-attacks."

Paragraph 68, 29th April: "The enemy's advance stayed." "On the British front the positions held by the 21st, 49th and 25th Divisions were strongly attacked between 5 a.m. and 5.30 a.m. On the failure of these attacks bodies of German infantry advanced at 6 a.m. in mass formation with bayonets fixed against the 49th Division and were repulsed with the heaviest losses. . . .

"During the morning repeated attacks were made without result against the 25th and the 49th. . . . At all points the attack was pressed vigorously with massed bodies of troops and the losses suffered by the German infantry were very great. Throughout the whole of the fighting our infantry and artillery fought magnificently, and in more than one instance our troops went out to meet the German attack and drove back the enemy with the bayonet. At the end of the day except for a small loss of ground at Voormezeele our line was intact and the enemy had undergone a severe and decided check." The French retook Locre on the 30th, and the enemy's great offensive was ended.

On 2nd May telegrams, sent by Sir Douglas Haig to the G.O.C. Second Army, congratulating certain divisions, were published. One of these

56 THE TERRITORIAL DIVISIONS

referred to the 49th Division and was as follows: " I desire to express my appreciation of the very valuable and gallant service performed by troops of the 49th Division since its entry into the battle north of Armentières. The courage and determination shown by this Division have played no small part in checking the enemy's advance, and I wish you to convey to the General Officer Commanding, and to all officers and men under his command, my thanks for all that they have done."

Sir Douglas Haig several times, in the course of his written despatch, refers to the splendid conduct of the troops engaged in the Lys battle. The enemy employed 42 divisions of which 33 were "fresh," while 9 had come from the Somme. The British had 25 divisions of which only 8 had not been in the furnace of the Somme. Further it has to be kept in view that, as many divisions were sent from the northern to the southern area during the March retreat, the work of and strain upon those left in the north, such as the 49th, were greatly increased: these were thus not "fresh" in the sense that the enemy's forces were "fresh." French assistance was of the utmost value in finally convincing the enemy that his offensive was a failure, but that assistance could not come until after the battle had raged for a full week.

In paragraph 70 Sir Douglas Haig remarked: "Both by them (the divisions brought from the Somme) and by the divisions freshly engaged every yard of ground was fiercely disputed, until troops were overwhelmed or ordered to withdraw. Such withdrawals as were deemed necessary in the course of the battle were carried out successfully and in good order.

"At no time, either on the Somme or on the Lys, was there anything approaching a breakdown of command or a failure of morale. Under conditions that made rest and sleep impossible for days together, and called incessantly for the greatest physical exertion and quickness of thought, officers and men remained undismayed, realising that for the time being they must play a waiting game, and determined to make the enemy pay the full price for the success which for the moment was his."

When one reads the detailed accounts of the work done by any of the divisions on the Lys one is filled with wonder and amazement at the power of endurance, the unbending and self-sacrificing spirit and technical efficiency of units, many of which had suffered a 50 per cent. loss a fortnight or less before the 9th April, and were to the extent of a full half composed of lads sent to France after 22nd March.

The 49th Division was moved to the south and joined the XXII. Corps at the end of August 1918. On 12th September they relieved the 51st in the Plouvain sector, east of Arras. They took part in the last great advance. Along with the Canadian Corps they were engaged in an attack on 11th October, north-east of Cambrai. On that date the fighting was stiff and the losses were severe, but on the 12th good progress was made. The advance continued on 20th October and the XXII. Corps drove the enemy across the Selle and the Écaillon

58 THE TERRITORIAL DIVISIONS

rivers and in the last week of October were up against the Rhonelle position.

In Sir Douglas Haig's despatch of 21st December, 1918, paragraph 49, the Battle of the Sambre, 1st to 11th November, he says: " During these two days, 1st and 2nd November, the 61st, 49th (Major-General N. J. G. Cameron) and 4th Divisions crossed the Rhonelle river, capturing Maresches and Preseau after a stubborn struggle, and established themselves on the high ground two miles to the east of it. On their left the 4th Canadian Division captured Valenciennes and made progress beyond the town. As a consequence of this defeat the enemy on the 3rd November withdrew on the Le Quesnoy—Valenciennes front."

The following battalions were chosen for the Army of the Rhine: 1/5th and 1/6th West Yorkshire Regiment, 1/5th Yorkshire Light Infantry and 1/4th York and Lancaster Regiment.[1]

---

[1] An account of some of the more important features in the history of the 49th Division and of its younger sister the 62nd will be found in *The West Riding Territorials in the Great War*, by Major L. Magnus (Kegan Paul and Co., 15s.). Some most impressive pictures of life in the Ypres salient and at Nieuport in 1917 are to be found in *Happy Days with the 47th and 49th Divisions*, by Benedict Williams (Harding and More, 1921, 7s. 6d.).

50TH (NORTHUMBRIAN) DIVISION

First Line

THE 50th Division will always be associated with the Second Battle of Ypres, now designated " The Battles of Ypres, 1915," which began on 22nd April, 1915, by a great discharge of gas, then seen and felt for the first time in warfare, and which lasted till 25th May. Their presence was of the utmost value when the British and French only held on with the very greatest difficulty and at tremendous cost. Some battalions of the Division had only arrived in France a few days before the commencement of the battle.

In his despatch of 31st May, 1915, Sir John French " mentioned " officers and men of the following battalions of the 50th Division: 4th, 5th and 6th Northumberland Fusiliers and 5th, 6th and 8th Durham Light Infantry.

In his despatch of 15th June which deals with the Second Battle of Ypres Sir John French said, paragraph 4: " During the night " (of the 22nd April) " I directed the Cavalry Corps and the Northumbrian Division, which was then in general reserve, to move to the west of Ypres, and placed these troops at the disposal of the General Officer commanding the Second Army."

The fighting on 22nd-23rd April is now the " Battle of Gravenstafel Ridge."

On the 24th April the 9th Durham Light Infantry

60 THE TERRITORIAL DIVISIONS

and other battalions of the Division had very heavy fighting. Several had been detached to assist the old Regular brigades to hold the line, and all the battalions of the 50th were in the thick of the struggle during the ensuing four weeks, either in their own brigades or attached to others. The pressure was so great and so continuous, and reserves so scanty, that even the Regular Divisions had constantly to detach units to help neighbours in distress. On 24th May when the enemy made his final big effort the 151st (Durham Light Infantry) Brigade were near Hooge and did most valuable and gallant service.

After describing the heavy and often " hand-to-hand " fighting on the 23rd, 24th and 25th April, when the enemy put forth his utmost strength to break the line, while it was yet dazed by the gas, Sir John French said, as to the 26th: " On the right of the Lahore Division the Northumberland Infantry Brigade " (the 149th) " advanced against St. Julien and actually succeeded in entering, and for a time occupying, the southern portion of the village. They were, however, eventually driven back, largely owing to gas, and finally occupied a line a short way to the south. This attack was most successfully and gallantly led by Brigadier-General Riddell, who, I regret to say, was killed during the progress of the operation."

Unfortunately the 151st Brigade was unable to support the attack as, at the time, they were engaged in assisting the 28th Division to repel an attack by the enemy further south, and the 150th were also fighting elsewhere. The fighting

FIFTIETH DIVISION

24th April—4th May is now the "Battle of St. Julien."

The losses of the Division were very heavy, exceeding 2500 in the first five days alone.

Towards the close of his despatch Sir John French mentioned that several Territorial Divisions had in the period under review been employed as divisional units and had "all borne an active and distinguished part, and had proved themselves thoroughly reliable and efficient."

Sir Douglas Haig's despatch of 23rd December, 1916, as to the Somme battle, paragraph 27 (Dent's edition, note and map, p. 41), shows that the 50th Division was employed in the attack of 15th September, officially the Battle of Flers-Courcelette, it being then in the III. Corps, Fourth Army. The attack was successful and a big gain of ground was made. The map opposite p. 43 shows that the Division was again in the attack of 25th and 26th September, the Battle of Morval, when another section of the German defensive system was bitten off.

During October the Division had, frequently, bitter fighting in the Eaucourt—Le Sars area, the Battle of the Transloy Ridges, when further ground was gained and made secure. Winter's arrival found them still in the mud of that much fought-for region.

The despatch of 25th December, 1917, dealing with the Battle of Arras, 1917, paragraph 18 (Dent's edition) as to 13th and 14th April, states: "In the centre a Northumberland Brigade of the 50th Division (Major-General P. S. Wilkinson), advancing in open order, carried the high ground east of Héninel and captured Wancourt Tower. Three counter-attacks against this position were successfully driven off and further ground was gained on the ridge south-east of Héninel." Officially this is the First Battle of the Scarpe, 1917.

Paragraph 21, as to the attack on 23rd April, the Second Battle of the Scarpe, 1917: " On the main front of attack good progress was made at first at almost all points. By 10 a.m. the remainder of the high ground west of Chérisy had been captured by the attacking English brigades (30th and 50th Divisions)." The enemy made many counter-attacks " in great force . . . and with the utmost determination regardless of the heavy losses inflicted by our fire." Part of the ground gained in the morning was lost in the afternoon but all was made good in another assault on the 24th after very fierce fighting. In the Arras battle the Division operated with the XVIII. and VII. Corps.

The Division was brought north in October and entered the line on the north side of the Ypres salient, where, as part of the XIV. Corps, they had an indescribably bad time amidst lakes of mud and water. Movement at the best could only be very slow, often it was impossible, and thus the losses of the attacking troops were rendered very heavy.

The despatch of 25th December, 1917, makes frequent reference to the adverse conditions. In paragraph 55 there is the following sentence: " The year was far spent. The weather had been consistently unpropitious, and the state of the ground, in consequence of the rain and shelling combined, made movement inconceivably difficult." After considering the various factors " affecting the problem,

FIFTIETH DIVISION 63

among them the desirability of assisting our Allies in the operations to be carried out by them on the 23rd October, in the neighbourhood of Malmaison, I decided to continue the offensive further and to renew the advance at the earliest possible moment consistent with adequate preparation." The Division formed part of the assaulting line on 26th October when ground was gained. This is officially designated the Second Battle of Passchendaele.

Much rain fell in October and it was only on ground above the general level that progress could be made in the various attacks undertaken.

The Division remained in the salient, chiefly between Houthulst Forest and Passchendaele, for the next three months.

The despatch of 20th July, 1918, deals with the German attack in the St. Quentin district which began on 21st March. Regarding the position west of St. Quentin, in the centre of the Fifth Army, on the 22nd, paragraph 22, Sir Douglas Haig said: " Our troops, fighting fiercely and continuously, were gradually forced out of the battle zone on the whole of this front and fell back through the 20th and 50th Divisions holding the third defensive zone . . . in the hope of re-organising behind them."

" By 5.30 p.m. the enemy had reached the third zone at different points and was attacking the 50th Division heavily between Villéveque and Boucly. Though holding an extended front of some 10,500 yards, the Division succeeded in checking the enemy's advance, and by a successful counter-attack drove him temporarily from the village of Coulaincourt. At the close of the engagement, however, the troops of the 50th Division about Pœuilly had been forced back, and by continued pressure along the south bank of the Omignon river the enemy had opened a gap between their right flank and the troops of the 61st Division." . . . At this gap strong bodies of German troops broke through the third defensive zone.

As all available reserves at the disposal of the Fifth Army had been thrown into the fight, the Army Commander at 11 p.m. on the 22nd issued orders to withdraw to the Somme. Paragraph 23: "These withdrawals were carried out under constant pressure from the enemy, covered by rearguards of the 20th, 50th and 39th Divisions which were continually in action with the German troops."

Paragraph 24 shows that on the 23rd, the Fifth Army Commander issued orders to cross to the west side of the Somme. In paragraph 26 it is stated that "Further north the withdrawal to the west bank of the Somme was carried out successfully during the morning and early afternoon, effectively covered by troops of the 50th Division. By 3.15 p.m. all troops were across the river, and the bridges, for the most part, destroyed." The operations 21st to 23rd March are now designated the Battle of St. Quentin.

Paragraph 43 deals with the fight for the Rosières line — the Battle of Rosières — 27th March. The 50th Division was in support of "a very gallant and successful counter-attack" by troops of the 8th Division.

Paragraph 47 describes the fighting in the Avre and Luce valleys, 29th, 30th and 31st March, and says: "In the evening" of the 30th, "a most successful counter-attack by troops of the 20th and 50th Divisions re-established our line south of the Luce and captured a number of prisoners."

Mr. Sparrow in his *Fifth Army* gives a very full account of the invaluable work of the 50th. He indicates the opinion that their task was made heavier than it need have been, through their having been kept by G.H.Q. too far from the battle zone, and they had thus to be thrown into a surging battle immediately after a long and most exhausting march. Probably there were good reasons why they should have been located where they were before the battle began. Mr. Sparrow states that the line which had to be held by the Division, 22nd–23rd March, was 4000 yards longer than the frontage mentioned in the despatch; at p. 108 he makes it 14,500 yards. The fighting was so severe and continuous that, by the evening of the 27th, the 4th and 5th Northumberland Fusiliers together could only muster 200 rifles (see p. 129). Other units of the Division were also reduced to mere shadows, which, however, struggled and fought till the line stabilised, although scarcely able to keep their limbs moving or their eyes open. Mr. Sparrow shows conclusively that never did human beings make a finer effort than did the Fifth Army between 21st March and the early days of April. That they were successful was almost a miracle and is a lasting tribute to the spirit of officers and men and the skill of their leader, General Gough.

When, in the beginning of April, it was seen that the German offensive from St. Quentin had been

66 THE TERRITORIAL DIVISIONS

stopped, several divisions, including the 50th, which during the last ten days of March had never been out of the awful struggle, were taken north to Flanders, as a quieter part of the line, where they might recuperate and assimilate their much needed drafts. Alas, they were to find themselves in another furnace.

The Lys battles are dealt with in the despatch of 20th July, 1918, and it will be remembered that these began with a great attack on the Portuguese sector on 9th April, spreading to that of the 40th Division on their left and that of the 55th at Givenchy on the right. The 50th had arrived at Merville behind the Portuguese on the 8th. Their artillery was not forward. The 51st, also just arrived from the Somme, were behind the 55th. On the morning of the 9th the 50th deployed and were soon engaged, the 51st also moved forward. After the Portuguese front was broken in, the 55th succeeded in forming a defensive flank which bending to the west established touch with the 51st Division. On the left of the latter were the 50th, but this division was unable to establish touch with the 40th.

In paragraph 51 Sir Douglas Haig said: "During the afternoon troops of the 51st and 50th Divisions (chiefly composed of drafts hurriedly sent up to join their regiments) were heavily engaged east of the Lawe river and were gradually pressed back upon the river crossings. The enemy brought up guns to close range, and in the evening crossed at Estaires and Pont Riqueul, but in both cases was driven back by counter-attacks."

In paragraph 53, the struggle for Estaires, Sir

Douglas said: "Early in the morning of the 10th April the enemy launched heavy attacks covered by artillery fire about the river crossings at Lestrem and Estaires, and succeeded in reaching the left bank at both places; but in each case he was driven back again by determined counter-attacks by the 50th Division.

"The enemy continued to exercise great pressure at Estaires and fierce street fighting took place, in which both sides lost heavily. Machine guns mounted by our troops in the upper rooms of houses did great execution on his troops as they moved up to the attack, until the machine guns were knocked out by artillery fire. In the evening the German infantry once more forced their way into Estaires, and after a most gallant resistance the 50th Division withdrew at nightfall to a prepared position to the north and west of the town. East of Estaires" (apparently outside the area of the 50th) "the enemy had already crossed the Lys in strength."

In paragraph 56, as to events on the 11th, he said: "At Estaires, the troops of the 50th Division, tired and reduced in numbers by the exceptionally heavy fighting of the previous three weeks, and threatened on their right flank by the enemy's advance, south of the Lys, were heavily engaged. After holding their positions with great gallantry during the morning they were slowly pressed back in the direction of Merville. The enemy employed large forces on this front in close formation and the losses inflicted by our rifle and machine-gun fire were unusually heavy. Our own troops, however,

68 THE TERRITORIAL DIVISIONS

were not in sufficient numbers to hold up his advance," etc. Portions of the Division continued in the fighting line throughout the 12th and 13th April.

Paragraph 58: "Though our troops had not been able to prevent the enemy's entry into Merville their vigorous resistance combined with the maintenance of our positions at Givenchy and Festubert had given an opportunity for reinforcements to build up our line in this sector."

The sacrifices of the 50th Division, which were again very great, were not in vain.

In the supplementary despatch of 23rd April, 1918, as to work of certain divisions, Sir Douglas Haig said: "The 50th Division, though but recently withdrawn from a week of continuous fighting south of the Somme, on April 9th and subsequent days held up the enemy along the line of the Lys, and by the stubbornness of its resistance at Estaires and Merville checked his advance until further reinforcements could be brought up."[1]

The despatch of 21st December, 1918, paragraph 10, shows that the 50th along with the 8th, 21st, 25th and 19th Divisions, all very recently engaged in the struggles in northern France and Flanders, composed largely of young drafts and "in no condition to take part in major operations until they had had several weeks' rest," formed the IX. British Corps which was sent to the Aisne in May 1918, and was involved in the "intense fighting," when the enemy, employing 28 divisions, commenced his attack on the

[1] As to the Lys battle see also 49th, 51st, 55th and 61st Divisions.

FIFTIETH DIVISION 69

French Sixth Army on the 27th of that month. The attacks continued till 6th June, the Franco-British line being forced back. " Throughout this long period of incessant fighting against greatly superior numbers the behaviour of all arms of the British forces engaged was magnificent. What they achieved is best described in the words of the French General under whose orders they came, who wrote of them: 'They have enabled us to establish a barrier against which the hostile waves have beaten and shattered themselves. This none of the French who witnessed it will ever forget.' "

In *The History of the 25th Division*, p. 250, speaking of their arrival in Champagne, there occurs the following sentences: " To the few in the 25th Division who had served with the original British Expeditionary Force in August and September, 1914, the district brought memories of the Battle of the Marne and the subsequent advance to the Aisne; but no hint was given of the extent of the tragedy shortly to be enacted over this historic ground.

" The front of about 24,000 yards held by the IX. British Corps ran along the high ground about four miles north of the Aisne for the first " (left) " 16,000 yards gradually bending S.E., on its right, to the important point of Berry-au-Bac, where the line crossed the river and continued on S.E. in the direction of Rheims for another 8000 yards. The right sector south of the Aisne was held by the 21st Division, in touch with the 36th French Division on its right; the 8th Division in the centre, and the 50th Division to the left, joining up with the 22nd

70 THE TERRITORIAL DIVISIONS

French Division of the XI. French Corps, north of Craonne."

The 50th, according to all accounts, put up a glorious defence. Its position made a withdrawal impracticable, even if that had been contemplated; it was overwhelmed where it stood. As a fighting force the Division was practically destroyed; to it little more remained than the splendid tradition it had created.

Sir Arthur Conan Doyle, vol. v., chapter xi., gives an excellent description, with many interesting details, of the magnificent stand made on 27th May, by the 50th, 8th, and 21st Divisions, aided each by a brigade of the 25th, and of the intense fighting which occurred down to 6th June when the enemy's effort was spent. As on the Somme and Lys, his losses had been enormous. The 19th Division came into the line on the 29th May, when prospects were very gloomy, and their presence did much to establish a new line. On 6th June the 4th Shropshire, T.F., of the 19th Division gained the Croix de Guerre, with palms for the recapture of Mont Bligny.

A well-founded claim might be put forward that history records no instance where a large body of troops has come through, without loss of morale or fighting spirit, three such ordeals, within less than three months, as were endured by the divisions composing the British IX. Corps on the Aisne. Although one of them, the 8th, had not been on the Lys, it had very heavy fighting about Villers Bretonneux, which it assisted to recapture 24th/25th April, three weeks after the close of the March battle. The other divisions were in all three struggles.

FIFTIETH DIVISION

Whereas in old days a battle ended within twelve, or on exceptional occasions within forty-eight hours of its commencement, the St. Quentin—Somme battle, generally known as the March Retreat, raged night and day without cessation for ten days, that on the Lys for nearly three weeks, and that on the Aisne for over a week. The question will probably be discussed by the military historian or essayist of the future.

Before the "Advance to Victory" was commenced the 50th Division had been reconstituted. The battalions which had been destroyed were replaced as follows:—149th Brigade: 3rd Royal Fusiliers, 13th Black Watch, 2nd Royal Dublin Fusiliers; 150th Brigade: 2nd Northumberland Fusiliers, 7th Wiltshire, 2nd Royal Munster Fusiliers; 151st Brigade: 6th Royal Inniskilling Fusiliers, 1st King's Own Yorkshire Light Infantry, 4th King's Royal Rifle Corps. See *Story of Fourth Army* (Hodder and Stoughton), p. 322.

The 50th was again to do fine work, the tradition held.

As part of the XIII. Corps, Fourth Army, the Division was employed in the last great British offensive, and played a part worthy of its past.

In the despatch of 21st December, 1918, paragraph 37, Sir Douglas Haig said: "On the 3rd October the Fourth Army attacked between Sequehart and Le Catelet and captured those villages and Ramicourt (see 46th Division) together with the Beaurevoir—Fonsomme line on that front. In this operation the 50th Division took Gouy and Le Catelet after heavy and prolonged fighting, in which a number of counter-attacks were beaten off." This is now the "Battle of the Beaurevoir Line," 3rd–5th October, 1918.

The XIII. Corps was again employed in the "Battle of Cambrai, 1918," on 8th and 9th October, and the 50th was engaged.

Paragraph 46 shows that the XIII. Corps employed the 50th and 66th Divisions in the successful "Battle for the Selle Crossings" 17th to 25th October. See also under 66th Division.

Paragraph 50, "The Battle of the Sambre," 1st to 11th November, states that the XIII. Corps was again engaged. On the 4th at 6.15 a.m. the Corps "attacked with the 25th, 50th and 18th Divisions and quickly overran the enemy positions despite strong opposition which at Preux-au-Bois was maintained until the village was completely surrounded by our infantry and tanks."

Major-General Montgomery in his *Story of the Fourth Army* deals with the fine work of the 50th on 3rd October, at p. 182, and as to another attack by the Division and other troops on the 8th, which was "an unqualified success," at p. 196.

On the 4th–5th November, the "Battle of the Sambre," the 50th had, in the clearing of the southern portion of the Mormal Forest, a very arduous task. It was difficult for the artillery to give adequate support owing to their movement being hampered by tree stumps and bogs.

After the 5th, the Division continued to advance. On the 7th, the Division captured Dourlers and on the 8th took Semousies and Floursies. On both days there was obstinate fighting. Regarding the 8th,

FIFTIETH DIVISION 73

Major-General Montgomery says, p. 259: "that the enemy selected the line of the Avesnes—Maubeuge road as a rearguard position. The vigour and determination of the attack, however, overcame all resistance." When the Armistice came on the 11th, the Division was east of the Avesnes—Maubeuge road.

The 50th was along with the 25th and other divisions in the IX. Corps on the Aisne, May 1918, and again were with the 25th in the XIII. Corps in the "Advance to Victory." There is much of interest regarding the work of both divisions in these operations in the excellent *History of the 25th*, by Colonel Kincaid-Smith (Harrison).

Apart from the first eight Regular divisions no British division had a longer spell of fighting than the 50th had, was in more of the big battles or came out of these with a better record.

The 1/9th Durham Light Infantry served with the 62nd Division in 1918 as Pioneers, but like other pioneer battalions, had frequently to use their weapons as well as their tools. The battalion was chosen for the Army of the Rhine, as was also the 1/5th Border Regiment which was originally "Army troops," but replaced the 1/7th Durham Light Infantry, taken out of the 50th to be a pioneer battalion.

Northumbria raised an enormous number of units in the earlier years of the war, and the second line Territorial Division was, like several others, sacrificed for draft-finding purposes. A number of garrison battalions, however, were formed and went abroad; of these there were selected for the

THE TERRITORIAL DIVISIONS

Armies of Occupation, etc.: Western Front, the 2/6th Durham Light Infantry; the Near East, the 2/5th and 2/9th Durham Light Infantry; Egypt, the 2/7th Northumberland Fusiliers; North Russia, the 2/7th Durham Light Infantry; Bermuda, the 2/4th East Yorkshire Regiment.

51ST (HIGHLAND) DIVISION

First Line

THE Division left Britain at the end of April and beginning of May 1915, and on arrival in France was immediately sent to the neighbourhood of the firing line.

Early in the year the Division had been bereft of six individual battalions for immediate service in France with regular divisions. The battalions which went out separately were replaced by a brigade of the 55th, West Lancashire, Division, which remained with the 51st till January 1916, and by the 6th and 7th Black Watch, battalions raised in the Highland divisional area but which, prior to 1914, were Army Troops. The two latter battalions remained permanently in the 51st Division.

The 8th Royal Scots, which sailed on 4th November, 1914, joined the 7th Division with which they took part in the stiff battles of Neuve Chapelle, 10th, 11th and 12th March, 1915, and Festubert, 15th to 18th May, 1915. For their good work on these and prior occasions six officers and four men were mentioned in the despatch of 31st May, 1915. The battalion, in August 1915, joined the 51st Division as pioneers. In the same despatch officers and men of the 4th Seaforths, 4th and 6th Gordon Highlanders and 4th Camerons were mentioned. The last-named belonged to the Division but

76 THE TERRITORIAL DIVISIONS

unfortunately did not serve with it except for about a month in the beginning of 1916.

The despatch of 15th June, 1915 (as to the Second Battle of Ypres, now "The Battles of Ypres, 1915," which commenced with the great gas attack on 22nd April and lasted till 25th May), paragraph 4, shows that the 7th Argyll and Sutherland Highlanders and 1st East Lancashire Regiment (10th Brigade) made a successful counter-attack on 8th May; for their good work two officers and three N.C.O.'s and men of the Argylls were mentioned. On the 10th the 9th Royal Scots, afterwards in the 51st, with other troops, repulsed with heavy loss to the enemy an attack made under cover of gas. On the 11th "the Germans attacked in force and gained a footing in part of the trenches, but were promptly ejected by a supporting company of the 9th Royal Scots." Unofficial writers have paid tribute to the splendid fighting spirit of these two battalions, the 7th Argylls and 9th Royal Scots, but the price had to be paid. Sir A. Conan Doyle remarks that on 24th May, 1915, towards the close of the battle, of the 7th Argylls there remained only two officers and 76 other ranks.

On 24th May at 2.45 a.m. the 9th Argyll and Sutherland Highlanders and other troops were "overcome with gas," and pressed back, "in a most determined attack."

In the same despatch, paragraph 5, as to the advance near Neuve Chapelle and Festubert, Sir John French remarked that on 17th May he gave orders "for the 51st (Highland) Division to move into the neighbourhood of Estaires to be ready to support

FIFTY-FIRST DIVISION 77

the operations of the First Army," and that on the 19th the 2nd Division was relieved by the 51st Division. On the 22nd the Division was " attached to the Indian Corps." Between the 18th May and the beginning of June the Division worked hard at consolidating the ground recently gained.

On 15th June the 51st along with the Canadians and 7th Division took part in an attack near Givenchy which met with little success. The casualties of the Division could not be called slight.

In July 1915 the Division was ordered to join the X. Corps, Third Army, and on the last days of the month took over from a French Division a section about Hamel near the Ancre.

About this time the Division seems to have gained the confidence of G.H.Q., as in August and later various New Army Divisions were attached to it for instruction, including the 18th, 22nd, 32nd, etc.

In January 1916 the Lancashire Brigade left to join their own Division and the 51st received the 9th Royal Scots, 4th Seaforths, 4th Gordon Highlanders and 7th Argyll and Sutherland Highlanders.

Sir Douglas Haig's despatch of 23rd December, 1916, which deals with the Somme Battle, paragraph 17 (Dent's edition), mentioned various engagements, now called the " Battle of Bazentin Ridge," in the latter half of July. "That evening (24th July) after heavy artillery preparation, the enemy launched two more powerful counter-attacks, the one directed against our new position in and around High Wood (51st Division, Major-General G. M. Harper) and the other delivered from the north-west of Delville Wood. Both attacks were completely broken up with very heavy losses to the enemy." The Division had attacked on the 22nd–23rd but had failed to gain much ground.

Paragraph 19 and note: Early in August the 51st, along with other divisions, was in other operations "involving much fierce and obstinate fighting," by which the line was pushed forward. About the 7th of August the Division was relieved and taken to Armentières. In the beginning of October the Division again went south, at first to Hebuterne and on the 17th to Beaumont Hamel.

Paragraph 33 and note, also 35 and 36 of the despatch, show that the 51st along with other troops took part in the attack on the Beaumont Hamel—St. Pierre Divion position on 13th November, now the "Battle of the Ancre, 1916." In a note to paragraph 33 it is remarked: "As the season advanced and the bad weather continued the scope of our plan had constantly to be reduced, until finally it was only possible to undertake the much more limited operation of the 13th November against Beaumont Hamel. The brilliant success of this attack, carried out as it was under most difficult conditions of ground, affords some indication of what might have been accomplished had the weather permitted us to give fuller effect to our original plan." The 51st Division captured the village, which was very strongly fortified, and over 2000 prisoners, their own losses being about 2500.

The "brilliant success" of the Division in the Beaumont Hamel battle brought it fame which was to endure and increase as the years of the war rolled on.

FIFTY-FIRST DIVISION 79

During December 1916, and part of January 1917, the Division was in the Courcelette sector where things were far from peaceful and hardships were extreme. In February they moved north to Arras, and remained there till the Battle of Arras.

The despatch of 25th December, 1917, paragraphs 13 and 14, and note to paragraph 13 (Dent's edition), describes the opening stages of the Battles of Arras which began on 9th April, 1917. The 51st, then in the XVII. Corps, Third Army, attacked east of Roclincourt, north-east of Arras; they were near the left of the line and next the Canadians whose task it was to seize the main Vimy Ridge. The 51st and its neighbour on the right, the 34th, had heavy fighting. "Their advance was delayed, not checked." The whole attack on the 9th was a great success. The fighting between the 9th and 14th is now the First Battle of the Scarpe, 1917. On the 12th the Division left the line, re-entering it on the 15th–16th and remaining in the battle till the 24th–25th.

Paragraph 21 deals with a big attack which our troops made on 23rd April on a front of nine miles, the Second Battle of the Scarpe, 1917. "North of the Scarpe Highland Territorials (51st Division) were engaged in heavy fighting on the western outskirts of Rœux Wood and the chemical works." "During the afternoon many counter-attacks developed all along the line and were repeated by the enemy with the utmost determination regardless of the heavy losses inflicted by our fire." "North of the Scarpe fierce fighting continued for the possession of Rœux, the chemical works and the station to the north without producing any lasting change

80 THE TERRITORIAL DIVISIONS

in the situation." The attack was renewed on the 24th and more progress was then made, the enemy's resistance weakening. For their "splendid" work on the 23rd, the Division was thanked and congratulated by the Corps and Army Commanders.

The losses of the Division during April amounted to about 4500.

Paragraph 27, as to the fighting in May, Third Battle of the Scarpe, 1917: "On the night of the 13th–14th our troops (51st Division) captured Rœux." The Division drove back some very heavy counter-attacks. Fighting continued for some days. The Army Commander again wired to the Division his congratulations "on their great gallantry at Rœux and the chemical works."

The Division was relieved on the 31st May, and a few days later was taken to the Ypres sector, there to refit and prepare for another great battle.

Paragraph 41 of the despatch deals with the assault by the British troops on 31st July, 1917, the "Battle of Pilckem Ridge" at the beginning of the Third Battle of Ypres. The note in Messrs. Dent's edition, p. 113, gives a list of the divisions employed. Among these is the 51st, then in the XVIII. Corps, Fifth Army. They were near the left of the British line. "Highland Territorials (51st Division) Welsh and Guards battalions secured the crossings of the Steenbeek." All objectives were taken early in the day. The losses of the Division were about 1600 and they took about 650 prisoners.

Paragraph 50 describes a successful attack made on 20th September: "North of the Zonnebeke—Langemarck Road, London and Highland Terri-

FIFTY-FIRST DIVISION 81

torials (58th and 51st Divisions) gained the whole of their objectives by midday though stiff fighting took place for a number of farms and strong places."

This action is now the Battle of the Menin Road Ridge. The losses of the Division were 1150.

The Division received the congratulations of the Corps and Army commanders on their work in the Ypres battles. In his message the Corps Commander said: " I venture to place it among the three best fighting divisions I have met in France during the past three years."

About this time the enemy published a statement that the 51st was the "most formidable division on the Western Front."

In the beginning of October the Division was back in the area south-east of Arras.

The despatch of 20th February, 1918, paragraph 3, shows that the 51st Division was part of the attacking force at the Battle of Cambrai, 1917, which commenced on 20th November, 1917. After mentioning the capture of Ribécourt by the 6th Division and the storming of Havrincourt by the 62nd, Sir Douglas Haig said: " The capture of these two villages secured the flanks of the 51st (Highland) Division (T.), Major-General G. M. Harper, advancing on the left centre of our attack up the slopes of Flesquières Hill against the German trench lines on the southern side of Flesquières village. Here very heavy fighting took place. The stout brick wall skirting the Château grounds opposed a formidable obstacle to our advance, while German machine guns swept the approaches. A number

82 THE TERRITORIAL DIVISIONS

of tanks were knocked out by direct hits from German field batteries in position beyond the crest of the hill. None the less, with the exception of the village itself, our second objectives in this area were gained before midday." Paragraph 4: "On the morning of the 21st November, the attack on Flesquières was resumed, and by 8 a.m. the village had been turned from the north-west and captured." "Following upon the capture of Flesquières, the 51st and 62nd Divisions, in co-operation with a number of tanks and squadrons of the 1st Cavalry Division, attacked at 10.30 a.m. in the direction of Fontaine-Notre-Dame and Bourlon. In this attack the capture of Anneux was completed, and, early in the afternoon, Cantaing was seized with some hundreds of prisoners. Progress was made on the outskirts of Bourlon Wood and, late in the afternoon, Fontaine-Notre-Dame was taken by the troops of the 51st Division and tanks."

The last-mentioned village was lost on the following day, see paragraph 6.

Paragraph 7: "On the morning of the 23rd November the 51st Division, supported by tanks, attacked Fontaine-Notre-Dame, but was unable to force an entrance. Early in the afternoon this Division repeated its attack from the west, and a number of tanks entered Fontaine, where they remained till dusk, inflicting considerable loss on the enemy. We did not succeed, however, in clearing the village, and at the end of the day no progress had been made on this part of our front."

On the 27th the Guards Division, which had relieved the 51st, again entered the much fought-

FIFTY-FIRST DIVISION 83

for village, but it was partly commanded by the Bourlon ridge and could not be held.

The 51st were not in the line on the 30th when the German counter-offensive took place. See 47th, 55th and 56th Divisions.

In the Cambrai battle the casualties of the Division were 1570. They took 2690 unwounded prisoners.

The great German offensive of March 1918 is dealt with in the despatch of 20th July, 1918. The 51st Division were then in the IV. Corps, Third Army, and were holding front line positions near Hermies, west of the Flesquières salient. On their right was the 17th Division of the V. Corps and on their left, about Lagnicourt, the 6th Division of the IV. Corps; see map opposite p. 186 of Messrs. Dent's edition of the *Despatches*.

In paragraph 16 Sir Douglas Haig, dealing with the 21st March, said: "On the Third Army front our line in the Flesquières salient had not been heavily attacked and was substantially intact. Beyond this sector fierce fighting took place around Demicourt and Doignies, and north of the village of Baumetz-lez-Cambrai. In this area the 51st Division, under the command of Major-General G. T. C. Carter-Campbell, was heavily engaged, but from noon onwards practically no progress was made by the enemy."

In his telegraphic despatch of 22nd March, after referring to the exceptional gallantry of the 24th and 3rd Divisions, Sir Douglas Haig said: " A very gallant fight was made by the 51st Division also, in the neighbourhood of the Bapaume—Cambrai road, against repeated attacks."

G

84 THE TERRITORIAL DIVISIONS

In paragraph 21 of the written despatch, dealing with the 22nd March, Sir Douglas Haig said: "In the neighbourhood of Baumetz the enemy continued his assaults with great determination, but was held by the 51st Division and a brigade of the 25th Division until the evening. Our troops were then withdrawn, under orders, to positions south of the village."

The fighting between 21st and 23rd March is now the Battle of St. Quentin, and that on 24th–25th March, the First Battle of Bapaume.

During the next few days the 51st Division fought many critical rearguard actions. It was thereafter taken out of the line. Its total losses since the morning of the 21st were over 4900.

About 1st April the Division entrained for the Bethune area and it was hoped that things would be quieter there; that hope was quickly to be blasted.

The same despatch deals with the German offensive in Flanders which commenced on 9th April. See also 49th, 50th, 55th and 61st Divisions.

Paragraph 51 deals with the opening of the Lys battle on 9th April. It is there stated: "Meanwhile, shortly after the opening of the bombardment, orders had been given to the 51st and 50th Divisions to move up behind Richebourg-St.-Vaast and Laventie and take up their positions in accordance with the pre-arranged defence scheme. Both these divisions had also been heavily engaged in the Somme battle, and had but recently arrived in the neighbourhood." In the course of the forenoon, when the left of the 55th Division had to move back to form a defensive flank, touch was established with the 51st. The 1st

King Edward's Horse and 11th Cyclist Battalion who had covered the deployment of the 51st and 50th occupied Lacouture, etc.," and " by their splendid defence of these places enabled troops of the 51st and 50th Divisions to come into action east of the Lawe river between Le Touret and Estaires." A quotation as to the heavy fighting which took place during the afternoon of the 9th has already been given under the 50th, and some remarks by Sir Douglas Haig as to the splendid bearing of the divisions in the Lys battle have been given under the 49th.

In his telegraphic despatch of 11th April, Sir Douglas Haig said that " the 51st Division had beaten off incessant attacks with great loss to the enemy and, by vigorous and successful counter-attacks had recaptured positions into which the enemy had forced his way."

Paragraph 58 of the written despatch shows that by a sudden attack just before dawn on April 12th the enemy broke through the left centre of the 51st Division about Pacaut and Diez du Vinage," but with the arrival of reinforcements " the enemy's progress in this sector of the front was definitely checked."

The Division had over 2500 casualties in the Lys battles. In a congratulatory message to the Division, dated 16th April, the First Army Commander said, " You have done wonders."

About the beginning of May the Division moved to the area east of Arras and remained about Oppy till 11th July. Here they had a comparatively quiet time.

86 THE TERRITORIAL DIVISIONS

The despatch of 21st December, 1918, paragraphs 11 and 12, deals with the assistance afforded by the British to their Allies in the Second Battle of the Marne. It shows that the XXII. Corps, Lieut-General Sir A. Godley, comprising the 15th, 34th, 51st and 62nd Divisions, were sent south in July. The two latter went to the east side of the salient. Paragraph 12 says: "On the 20th July, the 51st and 62nd Divisions of the XXII. Corps, attacked in conjunction with the French on the eastern side of the salient, south-west of Reims. The sector assigned to the British troops covered a front of 8000 yards, astride the Ardre river, and consisted of an open valley bottom, with steep wooded slopes on either side. Both valley and slopes were studded with villages and hamlets, which were for the most part intact, and afforded excellent cover for the enemy. On this front our troops were engaged for a period of ten days in continuous fighting of a most difficult and trying nature. Throughout this period steady progress was made, in the face of vigorous and determined resistance. Marfaux was taken on the 23rd July and on the 28th British troops retook the Montagne de Bligny which other British troops had defended with so much gallantry and success two months previously. In these operations, throughout which French artillery and tanks rendered invaluable assistance, the 51st and 62nd Divisions took 1200 prisoners from seven different German divisions and successfully completed an advance of over four miles." This is now designated the "Battle of Tardenois."

General Berthelot, commanding the Fifth French

FIFTY-FIRST DIVISION 87

Army, issued on 1st August an eloquent Order of the Day as to the work of the two divisions, in which the British had made the Valley of the Ardre their own, "bountifully watered with their blood." He mentioned that in addition to the prisoners 140 machine guns and 40 guns had been captured. "You, one and all, have added a glorious page to your history. Marfaux, Chaumuzy and the Montagne Bligny, these splendid words will be written in letters of gold in the annals of your regiments. Your French friends will remember your marvellous bravery and your perfect comradeship in arms." Later, General Guillaumat, then commanding the Fifth Army, bestowed on the 6th Battalion, Black Watch, Royal Highlanders (Perthshire), the exceptionally high honour of being "cité à l'Ordre de l'Armée" as follows:—

THE 6TH BATTALION ROYAL HIGHLANDERS

"This battalion *d'élite*, under the forceful command of Lieutenant Colonel Francis Rowland Tarleton, has given proof of splendid spirit and dash in the course of the hard fought battles between July 20th and 30th, 1918. After seven days of bloody fighting, in spite of exhaustion and the heavy losses caused by intense enemy machine-gun fire, it successfully stormed a wood strongly fortified and stubbornly defended by the enemy."

The losses of the 51st in July amounted to about 3900.

Both divisions were brought north to take part in the last British offensive commencing in August. In the supplementary despatch of 13th September,

1918, as to the work of certain divisions, Sir Douglas Haig said: " The 51st Division after taking part in both the Somme and Lys battles of March and April, and also in the French offensive south-west of Reims, on August 26th attacked north of the Scarpe, and in five days of successful fighting captured Rœux, Greenland Hill and Plouvain." The despatch of 21st December, 1918, paragraph 27, deals with the Battle of the Scarpe, 26th August to 3rd September, and shows that at that time the 51st was serving in General Sir Henry Horne's First Army, along with the Canadian Corps, who fought on their right. The incidents abovementioned are again dealt with.

The Division's losses in the Greenland Hill operations amounted to 1145. For their fine work they were congratulated and thanked by the Commander of the Canadian Corps, under whose orders they were in the Scarpe battle.

About the end of August and beginning of September the XXII. Corps took over on the north and south sides of the Scarpe and the 51st Division became part of that Corps. In the beginning of October the Corps moved to the south of the Canadian Corps and took part in what is now the '· Battle of Cambrai, 1918," 8th–9th October, with pursuit to the Selle, 9th–12th October, and on 11th October an advance towards the Selle river was commenced. On the 12th and 13th, the 51st had hard fighting. The attack was renewed on the 19th when there were signs of the enemy retiring, and he was closely pressed. The 51st took a prominent part, until the 29th of October, in various

FIFTY-FIRST DIVISION 89

actions which involved bitter fighting. For a most gallant charge against a counter-attack by the enemy, the 6th Argyll and Sutherland Highlanders, who had rejoined the 51st in October after two years' service as Pioneers to the 5th Division, were complimented by the Corps Commander.

Paragraphs 46 and 47 of the despatch deal with the Battle of the Selle River, 17th–25th October, and show that the 51st, as part of the XXII. Corps, First Army, were on the left of the attack on 24th October. The telegraphic despatches stated that the Division had sharp fighting on the 24th and again on the 27th when they repulsed a determined counter-attack near Maing with the bayonet. Their losses during October were 2835.

At the end of October the Division went out of the line to rest, and its very distinguished fighting career was closed.

Scottish regiments were, at various times during the war, in debt to the Midlands of England for drafts of young soldiers, who soon got the *esprit de corps* of their Scottish units. This debt was, partly at least, repaid when brigades were cut down to three battalions in the beginning of 1918. At that time the 51st gave to the 61st (South Midland) Division, three of its best battalions, the 9th Royal Scots, 5th Gordons, and 8th Argyll and Sutherland Highlanders. These formed the 183rd Brigade; and, in his detailed description of the awful struggle during the March Retreat, Battle of St. Quentin, Sir Arthur Conan Doyle gives the greatest possible credit to this brigade. The whole Division did splendid work in the St. Quentin battle, and also in the Lys battles in April. See 61st Division.

After the close of the Lys battles these three battalions were taken from the 61st and, at Arras, joined the 15th, Scottish, New Army, Division, which at Loos had earned a reputation it never lost. In July the 15th, as part of the XXII. Corps, went to the south-west of Soissons, in the French area, and came under the command of General Mangin for the great counter-attack on the German salient, which began on 18th July—the turning-point or day of the War. All three battalions played a notable part in the Buzancy battle on 28th July and following days, and paid their full share of the price for the great distinction earned by the 15th Division on that occasion. No higher compliment could have been paid by an Ally than the erection, by the French 17th Division, of the monument at Buzancy to the fallen of the 15th Division. See paragraph 12 of the despatch of 21st December, 1918, and note in Messrs. Dent's edition.

After Buzancy the 15th was taken to the Flanders border; its last great fight was past.

The following units of the 51st Division were chosen for the Armies of Occupation: 1/6th Black Watch, 1/4th and 1/5th Gordon Highlanders, and 1/8th Argyll and Sutherland Highlanders.

NOTE.—Since the foregoing account was written, and revised by two officers who served with the Division during the last three years of the war, the most excellent *History of the 51st Division*, by Major F. W. Bewsher (Blackwood and Sons), has been published. The "casualties suffered" have, with kind permission, been mainly taken from Major Bewsher's work.

52ND (LOWLAND) DIVISION
First Line

AFTER a long service on coast defence work in Scotland, the Division, in the last half of May, 1915, sailed for the Mediterranean and arrived at Alexandria early in June. Considerable intervals separated the dates of despatch of the various battalions to the Dardanelles, but the Division had practically all landed there before the first week of July closed.

The 156th Brigade, which disembarked 13th–16th June, was in time to take part in the action of 28th June. The Brigade was attached to the 29th Division and came into action on the right of the 87th Brigade.

The main object of the attack was to give the British more elbow room, our situation being still exceedingly cramped.

Sir Ian Hamilton, in his despatch of 26th August, 1915, states that the assault was entrusted to the VIII. Corps, Lieut-General A. G. Hunter-Weston. The 29th Division on the left had to carry the greatest extent of ground. "On the right of the 87th Brigade the 4th and 7th Royal Scots captured the further two Turkish trenches allotted to them, but further to the east, near the pivotal point, the remainder of the 156th Brigade was unable to get on." The ground gained was held against "repeated counter-attacks, which for many days and nights afterwards the enemy launched against the trenches they had lost."

The enemy trenches opposite the right front of the attack, near the pivotal point, had not been seriously bombarded by the artillery owing to shortage of shells. At that time a preliminary bombardment was a mere pretence when contrasted with what it became in 1917 or 1918, while the creeping barrage had not yet been devised. The 8th Battalion Scottish Rifles, the right battalion of the 156th Brigade, supported by the 7th Battalion, found themselves, as soon as they were "over the top," subjected to a murderous enfilade machine-gun fire from the right flank. Only a few unwounded men reached the opposing trenches, which were 175 yards distant. The 8th Battalion went in about 650 strong, they came out with one officer and 29 other ranks. One man who had reached the enemy position was captured. The ordeal of the battalion, in this its first action, seems to have been as severe as any experienced by an infantry battalion during the war.

The Turkish position at this point, H. 12, was attacked by another brigade soon afterwards. It remained intact, although the attackers suffered a loss of 1700.

In Sir Ian Hamilton's despatch of 11th December, 1915, he described the battle at Helles on 12th–13th July, and the Suvla Bay fighting in August. The action of 12th–13th July was supplementary to that of 28th June, the object being to push back the Turkish centre.

FIFTY-SECOND DIVISION

"On our right the attack was to be entrusted to the French Corps; on the right centre to the 52nd (Lowland) Division. On the 52nd Division's front the operation was planned to take place in two phases; our right was to attack in the morning, our left in the afternoon." The 29th Division was to make a diversion on the left. "At 7.35 a.m. after a heavy bombardment, the troops, French and Scottish, dashed out of their trenches, and at once captured two lines of enemy trenches." The 1st Division of the French Corps pushed forward and carried the whole forward system. "Further to the left the 2nd French Division and our 155th Brigade maintained the two lines of trenches they had gained. But on the left of the 155th Brigade the 4th Battalion King's Own Scottish Borderers pressed on too eagerly. They not only carried the third line of trenches, but charged on up the hill and beyond the third line, then advanced indeed until they came under the 'feu-de-barrage' of the French Artillery. Nothing could live under so cruel a cross fire from friend and foe, so the King's Own Scottish Borderers were forced to fall back with heavy losses to the second line of enemy trenches which they had captured in the first rush."

The second phase of the attack was launched as planned. "The 157th Brigade rushed forward under heavy machine-gun and rifle fire, and splendidly carried the whole of the enemy trenches allotted as their objective. Here then our line had advanced some 400 yards, while the 155th Brigade and the 2nd French Division had advanced between 200 and 300 yards. At six p.m. the 52nd Division

94 THE TERRITORIAL DIVISIONS

was ordered to make the line good. It seemed to be fairly within our grasp."

"All night long determined counter-attacks, one after another, were repulsed by the French and the 155th Brigade, but about 7.30 a.m. the right of the 157th Brigade gave way before a party of bombers and our grip upon the enemy began to weaken." Another attack at 3 p.m. on the 13th, in which the Royal Naval Division and French took part, met with success, and on the whole the line was greatly improved by the operations of the two days. "A solid and enduring advance had been achieved."[1]

Sir Ian Hamilton said: "The 1/5th Royal Scots Fusiliers commanded by Lieut-Colonel J. B. Pollok McCall; the 1/7th Royal Scots, commanded by Lieut.-Colonel W. C. Peebles; the 1/5th King's Own Scottish Borderers, commanded by Lieut.-Colonel W. J. Millar; and the 1/6th Highland Light Infantry, commanded by Major J. Anderson, are mentioned as having specially distinguished themselves in this engagement."

In his despatch of 6th March, 1916, which deals with the evacuation of the Gallipoli Peninsula, Sir C. C. Monro remarked: "Meanwhile the VIII. Corps had maintained the offensive spirit in bombing and minor operations with which they had

---

[1] In *The Fifth Highland Light Infantry*, 1914–18 (MacLehose and Co., 1921, p. 29), there is a statement that Sir Ian Hamilton had been misinformed as to the right of the 157th Brigade giving way before a party of bombers. It is admitted that a portion of trench had been vacated through an order having been misunderstood, but it is stated that another company at once occupied it and was holding it when the afternoon attack commenced. There may have been other incidents of which the "Fifth" were unaware.

FIFTY-SECOND DIVISION 95

established the moral superiority they enjoyed over the enemy. On the 29th December, the 52nd Division completed the excellent work which they had been carrying out for so long by capturing a considerable portion of the Turkish trenches, and by successfully holding these in the face of repeated counter-attacks."

The commander of the Division, Major-General the Hon. H. A. Lawrence, "was selected to take charge of all embarkation operations." The evacuation from Helles took place on the night of 8th January, 1916.

The 52nd Division was taken to Egypt. They crossed to the east side of the Suez Canal about the beginning of March, 1916, and they were to spend the ensuing twelve months in the desert of Sinai, their energies being consumed in assisting with railway construction and making and manning defensive posts.

In Sir A. Murray's despatch, dated 1st June, 1916, as to operations of the Egyptian force, between 10th January and 31st May, 1916, paragraph 8, after describing the attack on the Yeomanry at Oghratina and Qatia in the Sinai Peninsula on 23rd April, he says: "Meanwhile, at 5.30 a.m. a Turkish force, 1000 strong, with one gun, advancing from the south, attacked Dueidar, the most advanced defensible post, which was held by 100 men of the 5th Battalion, Royal Scots Fusiliers, under the command of Captain Roberts, 5th Battalion, Royal Scots Fusiliers. This officer, who throughout showed conspicuous skill and ability, succeeded in repelling two determined attacks on the position at 6.30 a.m. and 8.30 a.m. respectively.

96 THE TERRITORIAL DIVISIONS

Both attempts cost the enemy dear. At 9.30 a.m. reinforcements of two companies, 4th Royal Scots Fusiliers, under the command of Major Thompson, of that battalion, who had been despatched from Hill 70, seven miles away, on the first news of the attack, arrived at Dueidar. The various posts were strengthened and a counter-attack, delivered at 12.30 p.m. with great spirit, forced the enemy to retire, leaving 30 prisoners in our hands and 70 dead."

In his despatch of 1st October, 1916, Sir A. Murray dealt with operations in the desert east of the canal, in particular with the fighting on 3rd, 4th and 5th August, 1916, an attack by the Turks, the British counter-attack, etc. Paragraph 5: During the 4th, the enemy made several attacks against the Romani—Mahemdia defences, from the east, south and south-west. "These were repulsed by the garrisons, composed of Scottish and Welsh infantry, with considerable loss, and in spite of heavy artillery fire from the enemy's heavy howitzers, which in one or two cases inflicted severe casualties on our troops, who behaved with admirable steadiness." "Vigorous action, to the utmost limits of endurance, was ordered for the next day, and the troops, in spite of the heat, responded nobly. At daybreak the Scottish Territorial infantry, assisted by Australian and New Zealand mounted troops, took the remainder of Wellington Ridge by assault, capturing about 1500 prisoners."

Paragraph 6: "The Scottish troops, commanded by Major-General W. E. B. Smith, C.M.G., not only showed great steadiness under heavy artillery

FIFTY-SECOND DIVISION 97

fire, but were responsible for the assault which recaptured Wellington Ridge, on 4th August, and for clearing Abu Hamra on the 5th."

The troops mainly responsible for the recapture of the ridge were the 7th and 8th Scottish Rifles. These moved out from Romani, about two miles from the Ridge, at dusk on the 4th. The 7th, on the left, linked up with a work, 22a, garrisoned by the 5th Royal Scots Fusiliers. The 8th under Colonel Findlay pressed up the hill, and when the leading lines were about 50 yards from the crest they were fired on; they then dug in. The 7th moved forward until in line with the 8th. At dawn mounted troops came up on the right and about the same time a company of the 5th Royal Scots Fusiliers arrived. An assault had been ordered when the Turks surrendered. The 8th Scottish Rifles took 360 prisoners and the mounted troops prevented the remainder from escaping.

The fighting 4th–5th August is now designated the "Battle of Rumani."

The Division was in reserve in the first Battle of Gaza on 26th March, 1917 (see 53rd Division), but had stiff fighting in the second attempt made by Sir A. Murray's force to capture Gaza on 17th–19th April, 1917.

The despatch of 28th June, 1917, paragraph 9, shows that on 17th April the 52nd Division was in the centre, the 53rd on the left and the 54th on the right. The Abbas—Mansura ridge was seized by the 157th Brigade of the 52nd Division, with little opposition, and preparation was made for a further advance on the 19th. The arrangement of the divisions was as on the 17th. The 52nd in the centre unfortunately found its task too heavy.

"The left brigade of the 52nd Division" (the only one, as stated in paragraph 10, which could with advantage be employed owing to the configuration of the ground) "made good Lees Hill, the nearest point to our line of the enemy defences on the Ali Muntar ridge by 8.15 a.m., but on advancing beyond the Lees Hill this brigade came under very heavy machine-gun fire from Outpost Hill, which checked its progress." At 10 a.m. a lunette on Outpost Hill was captured.

Later "the left brigade, 52nd Division, was shelled out of its position on Outpost Hill, but the position was most gallantly retaken on his own initiative by Major W. T. Forrest, M.C., K.O.S.B., subsequently killed, who collected a few men for the purpose. All further attempts to launch an attack from Outpost Hill were shattered by fire at their inception."

Paragraph 10: In the afternoon the position was that the 52nd could not advance. A large area of extremely broken ground had been made exceedingly strong by the enemy, and the nests of machine guns could not be located and destroyed. The attack was eventually abandoned, the British losses being about 7000 men, but all ground gained was consolidated and kept. The "left brigade" was the 155th, the 156th was on the right and the 157th in reserve. The capture of the objectives involved an advance of two miles, with little cover, and only moderate artillery support.

At paragraph 15 Sir A. Murray recorded his

FIFTY-SECOND DIVISION 99

appreciation of what his troops had done. "Particular commendation is due to the infantry—52nd, 53rd and 54th Divisions." "Under severe trial they have now given ample proof of the finest soldierly qualities."

Sir E. Allenby took over the command of the Egyptian Expeditionary Force on 28th June, 1917. In his despatch of 16th December, 1917, he recounts the progress of the operations which culminated in the surrender of Jerusalem. The Army had received increases of strength and this enabled the commander to deal with a wider front and to avoid a direct attack on Gaza. Beersheba at the other end of the line was taken on 31st October. The Lowland Division was second from the left of the British line, opposite Gaza.

The despatch, paragraph 9, states: "As Umbrella Hill flanked the advance against the Turkish works further west, it was decided to capture it by a preliminary operation, to take place four hours previous to the main attack. It was accordingly attacked and captured at 11 p.m. on November 1st, by a portion of the 52nd (Lowland) Division. This attack drew a heavy bombardment of Umbrella Hill itself and our front lines, which lasted for two hours, but ceased in time to allow the main attack, which was timed for 3 a.m., to form up without interference."

The 7th Scottish Rifles had the principal rôle in the capture of Umbrella Hill.

In the main attack almost all objectives were reached. Between the 1st and the 6th progress was made east of Gaza and on the 7th it was found that the fortress had been evacuated. The fighting 27th October–7th November is now the "Third Battle of Gaza."

The British at once pursued, the 52nd Division following the coast. In paragraph 15, Sir E. Allenby speaks " of the rapidity of our movement along the coast and the determination with which his rearguards on this flank had been pressed."

"The advanced guard of the 52nd (Lowland) Division had forced its way almost to Burkah on the 11th."

After describing the position taken up by the Turks the despatch states that an attack for the 13th November was arranged. "This Katrah—El-Mughar line forms a very strong position, and it was here that the enemy made his most determined resistance against the turning movement directed against his right flank. The capture of this position by the 52nd (Lowland) Division, assisted by a most dashing charge of mounted troops, who galloped across the plain under heavy fire and turned the enemy's position from the north, was a fine feat of arms. Some 1100 prisoners, 3 guns and many machine guns were taken here. After this the enemy resistance weakened, and by the evening his forces were retiring east and north."

"In fifteen days our force had advanced sixty miles on its right, and about forty on its left. It had driven a Turkish army of nine infantry divisions and one cavalry division out of a position in which it had been entrenched for six months, and had pursued it, giving battle whenever it attempted to stand, and inflicting on it losses amounting probably to nearly two-thirds of the enemy's original effectives. Over 9000 prisoners, about 80 guns, more than 100 machine guns, and very large quantities of ammunition and other stores had been captured."

It is pardonable to point out here that the infantry of Sir E. Allenby's army was up till April 1918 composed, to the extent of four-fifths, of Territorial Divisions.

Jaffa was occupied on 16th November, 1917.

The despatch, paragraph 17, states that the "52nd Division in nine days covered 69 miles." Much of this was over heavy sand or very poor tracks.

Paragraph 20 refers to various attacks by the Turks: there was "particularly heavy fighting" towards the close of November near El Burj, "but Yeomanry and Scottish troops successfully resisted all attacks and inflicted severe losses on the enemy." A large number of prisoners were taken. Officially the fighting, 17th–24th November, is now the "Battle of Nebi Samwil."

Jerusalem was surrendered to troops of the 53rd and 60th Divisions on 9th December. See also 53rd, 54th and 60th Divisions.

In his despatch of 18th September, 1918, Sir E. Allenby stated that his next operations were designed to increase the security of Jaffa and Jerusalem. To the XXI. Corps, 52nd and 54th Divisions, was assigned the task of increasing the distance, between Jaffa and the enemy, from three miles to eight miles

Paragraph 3: "The weather was unfavourable. Heavy rains made the roads deep in mud and brought down the streams."

Paragraph 4: "The chief obstacle lay in the

crossing of the Nahr El Auja. This river is only fordable in places and all approaches to it are overlooked from Sheikh Muannis and Khurbet Hadrah. At these places two spurs running from north to south terminate abruptly in steep slopes some 500 yards from the river." These two places "and the high ground overlooking the river had to be captured, as a preliminary to the general advance, in order that bridges might be built.

" The chief difficulty lay in concealing the collection and preparation of rafts and bridging material. All preparations were completed, however, without attracting the enemy's attention, and on the night of December 20th–21st, the 52nd Division crossed the river in three columns. The enemy was taken completely by surprise. The left column, fording the river near its mouth, at this point four feet deep, captured Tell Er Rekkeit, 4000 yards north of the river's mouth; the centre and right columns crossing on rafts, rushed Sheikh Muannis and Khurbet Hadrah at the point of the bayonet. By dawn a line from Khurbet Hadrah to Tell Er Rekkeit had been consolidated, and the enemy deprived of all observation from the north over the valley of the Nahr El Auja.

" The successful crossing of the Nahr El Auja reflects great credit on the 52nd (Lowland) Division. It involved considerable preparation, the details of which were thought out with care and precision. The sodden state of the ground and, on the night of the crossing, the swollen state of the river added to the difficulties, yet by dawn the whole of the infantry had crossed. The fact that the enemy were taken by surprise, and that all resistance was overcome with the bayonet without a shot being fired, bears testimony to the discipline of this Division. Eleven officers, including two battalion commanders, and 305 other ranks, and ten machine guns were captured in this operation."

Despite " considerable hostile shell fire " bridges were completed, and by dusk on the 21st the whole of the Divisional artillery had crossed. On the 22nd, the 54th captured certain villages, and the 52nd not only reached all their objectives but consolidated a line two miles beyond " to deny direct observation on Jaffa harbour to the enemy."

For their particularly fine work the 52nd received the congratulations of the Army, Corps and Divisional commanders. All three brigades shared in the work and the distinction it brought. The 155th took Khurbet Hadrah, the 156th Sheikh Muannis, and the 157th, the brigade which forded the river, captured Tell Er Rekkeit.

The fighting 21st–22nd December is now designated the " Battle of Jaffa."

At the close of the despatch, paragraph 15, Sir Edmund Allenby remarked that the 52nd Division embarked for France in the first week of April 1918. On 7th–8th May the Division took over a portion of the line east of Arras. They were now in the VIII. Corps under Commander Sir A. Hunter Weston, with whom they first fought at the Dardanelles. In the middle of August they moved further south to take a part in the big effort to be made there.

A quotation from Sir Douglas Haig's telegraphic

despatch of 13th September, 1918, as to good work by various divisions, which contains a reference to the 52nd attacking along with the 56th on 23rd August, is given under the 56th, London, Division.

In the despatch of 21st December, 1918, paragraph 22, Sir Douglas Haig mentioned that the 52nd was employed with the VI. Corps, Third Army, in the main attack on 23rd–24th August, a phase of the " Battle of Albert, 1918," in the sector north of Albert. " On the left of the 56th, the 52nd Division (Major-General J. Hill) took Hénin-sur-Cojeul and gained a footing in St.-Martin-sur-Cojeul."

Heavy fighting on 24th August and following days brought the 52nd into the Hindenburg line. On the 26th they made good progress on the north of the Cojeul and took Hénin Hill, getting well into the Hindenburg line, and moving down it on the 27th, they gave assistance to the 56th on their right.

The fighting in this area 26th–30th August is now officially designated the " Battle of the Scarpe, 1918."

After three days' rest the 52nd relieved the 56th and, on 1st September, cleared the famous Bullecourt, round which there had been a great struggle; as there was in April 1917. This was a necessary preliminary to a big attack fixed for the 2nd September.

Paragraph 28 of the despatch deals with " The storming of the Drocourt—Quéant line " on 2nd September. " The maze of trenches at the junction of that line and the Hindenburg system was stormed and the enemy was thrown into precipitate retreat on the whole front to the south of it. This gallant feat of arms was carried out by the Canadian Corps of the First Army," with " the 4th English Division, and the XVII. Corps of the Third Army, employing the 52nd, 57th and 63rd Divisions."

After referring to the fine work of the Canadian Corps, Sir Douglas Haig said: " On the right the attack of the XVII. Corps, launched, at the same hour by the 52nd and 57th Divisions, directed its main force on the triangle of fortifications, marking the junction of the Hindenburg and Drocourt—Quéant lines, north-west of the village of Quéant. Pressed with equal vigour it met with success equally complete. There was stern fighting in the net-work of trenches, both north and south of Quéant, in which neighbourhood the 52nd (Lowland) Division performed distinguished service, and, by the progress they made, greatly assisted our advance further north. Early in the afternoon our troops had cleared the triangle and the 63rd Division had passed through to exploit the success thus gained."

The fighting on 2nd-3rd September is now the " Battle of the Drocourt—Quéant line."

In a telegraphic despatch of 20th September Sir Douglas Haig said: " On the 17th a corporal and six men of the 1/5th Highland Light Infantry, 52nd Division, forming garrison of one of our posts just north of the village, were surrounded and believed to have been captured. During two days Germans held the village this party maintained their position and inflicted many casualties on the enemy. On the night of 19th-20th, when Mœuvres was retaken, the whole party regained their unit without loss."

The very gallant N.C.O. was awarded the Victoria Cross. The village was retaken by the 52nd Division.

The XVII. Corps was again employed on 27th September, "the Battle of Cambrai and the Hindenburg line." Paragraph 35 of the despatch states: "In the centre the 52nd Division, Major-General F. J. Marshall, passing its troops across the canal by bridgeheads previously established by the 57th Division,[1] on the opening of the assault, carried the German trench lines east of the canal and gained the high ground overlooking Graincourt."

The advance was continued successfully by the XVII. Corps between 27th September and 1st October, the 52nd doing particularly well, not only at the crossing of the Canal du Nord but in the capture of the heavily wired defences on either side of it.

The designation of the fighting 27th September–1st October, has been altered by the Nomenclature Committee and is now the "Battle of the Canal du Nord." They have fixed the dates of the "Battle of Cambrai, 1918," to be 8th and 9th October.

Early in October the Division left the XVII. Corps and later that month took over from the 12th Division in the VIII. Corps, Fifth Army.

With short intervals of rest the Division continued in the line of the advance until Armistice Day. They

[1] At page 281 of Messrs. Dent's edition of *Sir Douglas Haig's Despatches* the following note occurs at this point: "This is incorrect. There were no bridgeheads at this time and the crossings were forced by the 52nd Division at the opening of their attack."

FIFTY-SECOND DIVISION 107

crossed the Belgian frontier south of Péruvelz, and moving eastward by Sirault, were about ten miles north of Mons on 11th November. During these last few weeks there was frequently stubborn opposition which involved sharp fighting.

The 5th King's Own Scottish Borderers, 8th Scottish Rifles, and 5th Argyll and Sutherland Highlanders of the 52nd served during the last five months in the 34th Division (Major-General Nicholson), which after suffering heavy losses in the German offensive of March and April was reconstituted largely with battalions from the Palestine Divisions. It served with the French Tenth Army, south of Soissons in July 1918, and was highly complimented by General Mangin, the Army Commander. The battalions from the 52nd seem to have done exceptionally well both south of Soissons and at the capture of Gheluwe in Belgium, 14th October, and Anseghem, 31st October, when the 34th was advancing as part of the X. Corps, Second Army. The 34th Division reached Halluin.

The 5th and 6th battalions, Scottish Rifles, and 9th Highland Light Infantry lost their places in the Division through going to France early in the war. Indeed the 5th Scottish Rifles was one of the first Territorial battalions to be employed in that theatre, the 5th and 6th were eventually amalgamated. The fine work of all three battalions when in the 33rd Division was very frequently praised by unofficial historians.

These three units were replaced by the 4th and 7th Battalions, The Royal Scots, and the 5th Argyll and Sutherland Highlanders, all from "Army Troops."

The following units were selected for the Armies of Occupation on the Western Front: the 5/6th Royal Scots, which served as separate battalions in the Near East, the 5th Battalion landing at Helles with the 29th Division, and, after amalgamation, in France with the 32nd Division; the 1/4th Royal Scots Fusiliers; the 1/5th King's Own Scottish Borderers; the 5/6th Scottish Rifles; the 1/8th Scottish Rifles; and the 1/9th Highland Light Infantry.

The 32nd Division formed part of the Fourth Army throughout the "Advance to Victory." In Major-General Montgomery's *Story of the Fourth Army* there are several flattering references to the work of the 5/6th Royal Scots, as at p. 178, 3rd October, where he refers to their capture of Sequehart and its retention after the third time of capture —" partly also to the stubborn manner in which the 5/6th Royal Scots clung to the village it had three times captured."

53RD (WELSH) DIVISION
FIRST LINE

THE Division landed at Suvla Bay, Gallipoli, between 7th and 10th August, 1915, and became a part of the larger force which landed a few days earlier.

In his despatch of 11th December, 1915, Sir Ian Hamilton describes the attempt made on the 9th August by the 11th Division to seize hills north of Anafarta-Sagir. He remarked, "The line was later on prolonged by the remainder of the 34th Brigade and two battalions of the 159th Brigade of the 53rd Division. Their right was connected with the Chocolate Hills by the 33rd Brigade." "Some of the units which took part in this engagement acquitted themselves very bravely. I regret I have not had sufficient detail given me to mention them by name. The Divisional Commander speaks with appreciation of one freshly landed battalion of the 53rd Division, a Hereford battalion, presumably the 1/1st Herefordshire, which attacked with impetuosity and courage." "During the night of the 8th and 9th and early morning of the 9th the whole of the 53rd (Territorial) Division (my general reserve) had arrived and disembarked. . . . I had ordered it up to Suvla." "The infantry brigades of the 53rd Division (no artillery had accompanied it from England) reinforced the 11th Division."

The next paragraph shows that the 53rd Division took part in another attack on the 10th which failed. "Many of the battalions fought with great gallantry and were led forward with much devotion by their officers."

The 53rd Division along with the 54th were engaged on the 21st August, the "Battle of Scimitar Hill." They were to hold the enemy while the 29th and 11th Divisions attacked. The attack was not successful.

The troops at Suvla were evacuated in December 1915, the operation being successfully completed on the night of 19th–20th December.

The Division was taken to Egypt, and in his despatch of 1st June, 1916, paragraph 1, Sir A. Murray stated that the Division was early that year "occupied in operations on the Western Frontier of Egypt."

Sir A. Murray in his despatch of 1st October, 1916, paragraph 5, refers to the fighting in August, to the east of the Suez Canal, and a quotation as to the repulse of heavy attacks on 4th–5th August has already been given under the 52nd Division. This is now designated the "Battle of Rumani."

In his despatch of 28th June, 1917, paragraph 1, Sir A. Murray refers to the reconstitution of the "Desert Column" and mentions the 53rd Division as one of its units in March.

The Division bore a leading part in the "First Battle of Gaza," 26th–27th March, 1917. Paragraph 2 of the despatch last mentioned shows that

FIFTY-THIRD DIVISION

the 53rd Division was "to attack Gaza in front," their left being covered by the Gloucestershire Hussars among the sandhills on the coast. The approach march was made on the 25th and early on the 26th."

Paragraph 3: "Meanwhile the 53rd Division, under the command of Major-General A. G. Dallas, C.B., C.M.G., having thrown forward strong bridge-heads before dawn," (on the 26th) "crossed the Wadi Ghuzze at a point some three miles from the sea-coast, with one brigade on the right directed on the Mansura Ridge, and another brigade on the left directed on El Sheluf, some two miles south of Gaza, on the ridge running south-west from that place. A brigade was held in reserve." A brigade of the 54th was placed at the disposal of the G.O.C. 53rd Division when required.

"The deployment of the leading brigades commenced at 11.50 a.m., and the brigade in reserve moved forward shortly afterwards to its assigned position. In co-operation with artillery fire and long-range machine-gun fire, the brigade on the left pressed forward along the ridge, and the remaining brigades over the flat, open ground, practically devoid of cover. The final advance, which began just after 1 p.m., was very steady, and all the troops behaved magnificently, though the enemy offered a very stout resistance, both with rifle and machine-gun fire, and our advancing troops, during the approach march, the deployment and attack, were subjected to a heavy shrapnel fire."

In the afternoon the mounted troops attacked Gaza from north and north-east, and enveloped it, having heavy fighting among the gardens and enclosures.

112 THE TERRITORIAL DIVISIONS

Paragraph 4 : " Meanwhile the infantry attack was being pressed with great vigour, and by 4.30 p.m. considerable progress had been made. Portions of the enemy's positions were already in our hands and shortly afterwards the Ali Muntar Hill, a strong work known as the Labyrinth, and the ground in the immediate neighbourhood fell into our hands. The Australian and New Zealand Mounted Division was already exerting pressure on the enemy, and by 5 p.m. the enemy was holding out in the trenches and on the hill south of the Mosque only. The G.O.C. 53rd Division called on the brigade of the 54th Division (Brigadier-General W. Marriott-Dodington) which had been placed at his disposal to take this position. The brigade responded with the greatest gallantry in face of a heavy fire and after some hard fighting it pushed home its attack with complete success, so that when darkness fell the whole of the Ali Muntar position had been carried and a footing gained on the ridge to a point about 1200 yards north-east of that position."

Paragraph 5 deals with the " strong columns of the enemy " moving to the relief of Gaza, and other facts which compelled certain withdrawals to be undertaken.

In paragraph 6 occurs the sentence, " Nevertheless, though tired and ill-supplied with water the 53rd and 54th Divisions now placed under the G.O.C. 53rd remained throughout the day (27th) staunch and cheerful and perfectly capable of repulsing with heavy losses to the enemy any Turkish counter-attacks."

The Turks had been very strongly reinforced, and

although a strong counter-attack at 4 p.m. was shattered it was decided to retire to the west of the Wadi Ghuzze. This was carried out during the night.

At the close of paragraph 7 Sir A. Murray said: "The troops engaged, both cavalry, camelry and infantry, especially the 53rd Division and the brigade of the 54th, which had not been seriously in action since the evacuation of Suvla Bay at the end of 1915, fought with the utmost gallantry and endurance and showed to the full the splendid fighting qualities which they possess."

Paragraph 8 deals with the preparations for a second attack on the Gaza positions. For that operation the possession of the Wadi Ghuzze was necessary, so that the effort of 26th-27th March was not wasted.

The 17th April was the day fixed for the beginning of the second attack. In his despatch Sir A. Murray said, paragraph 9, that the "53rd Division, under the command of Major-General S. F. Mott, was to remain in position just north of the Wadi Ghuzze between the sea and the Gaza—Khan—Yunus road, but to carry out strong reconnaissances northward along the coast."

In the final stage of the attack "the 53rd Division was to attack the enemy's trenches in the sand-dunes south-west and west of Gaza, the line Sampson Ridge—Sheikh Ajlin being its first objective." The Division advanced at 7.15 a.m. on the 19th; "though meeting with considerable opposition, they gradually worked up to Sampson Ridge which was carried by a brigade early in the afternoon. This enabled another brigade to carry the high ground between this position and the coast with little opposition—and the first objective of the Division was attained."

At nightfall " the 53rd Division held the Sampson Ridge—Sheikh Ajlin line," but other parts of the force had not attained their objectives, casualties had been very heavy, about 7000, and the attack was abandoned. The ground gained was kept and consolidated. (See also 52nd and 54th Divisions.)

Sir E. Allenby assumed command of the Egyptian Expeditionary Force in June 1917, and the successful operations which began with the capture of Beersheba on 31st October, and ended with the surrender of Jerusalem on 9th December, are detailed in his despatch of 16th December, 1917.

The 53rd Division was, in these operations, on the right of the line. On 27th October the Turks attacked a line of outposts; paragraph 6: " The gallant resistance made by the Yeomanry enabled the 53rd (Welsh) Division to come up in time, and on their advance the Turks withdrew." On the same date the British bombardment of the Gaza defences commenced.

Paragraph 10, 1st November: The 53rd (Welsh) Division after a long march took up a position from six miles north of Beersheba to Muweileh. Between the 1st and 5th November the Division had sometimes heavy fighting.

Paragraph 11: " The 53rd (Welsh) Division had again had very severe fighting on the 6th. Their attack at dawn on Tel el Khuweilfeh was successful, and though they were driven off a hill by a counter-attack, they retook it and captured another

FIFTY-THIRD DIVISION 115

hill, which much improved their position. The Turkish losses in this area were very heavy indeed, and the stubborn fighting of the 53rd Division, the Imperial Camel Corps and part of the mounted troops during 2nd to 6th November drew in and exhausted the Turkish reserves, and paved the way for the success of the attack on Sheria. The 53rd Division took several hundred prisoners and some guns during this fighting."

The various actions 27th October to 7th November are now designated the "Third Battle of Gaza."

Paragraph 21: An attack on the Jerusalem defences was fixed for 8th December, the 53rd Division marched up the Hebron—Jerusalem road and met little opposition from the enemy. Heavy rains on the 7th and following days delayed the column but on the 9th "Welsh troops occupied a position east of Jerusalem across the Jericho road," the 60th Division being to the north of the city. At noon the city was surrendered. (See also 60th Division.)

In Sir E. Allenby's second despatch dated 18th September, 1918, he deals with the operations undertaken to provide more effectively for the security of Jerusalem and of Jaffa (see 52nd Division). The XX. Corps, including the 53rd and 60th Divisions, had been ordered to make an advance on a twelve-mile front to a depth of six miles north of Jerusalem, but in the meantime "the enemy attacked with great determination astride the Jerusalem—Nablus—Sechem road," on December 26th-27th. The 60th was heavily engaged but beat off the enemy with loss. Paragraph 5: "In

I

the meantime the enemy had delivered attacks against various points held by the 53rd Division east of Jerusalem. On the extreme right at Kh. Deir Ibn Obeid a company of Middlesex troops was surrounded by 700 Turks, supported by mountain artillery. Although without artillery support, it offered a most gallant resistance, holding out till relief came on the morning of the 28th. None of the other attacks on this division's front were any more successful." " By the evening of December 30th the XX. Corps had advanced on a front of twelve miles to a depth varying from six miles on the right to three miles on the left. This advance had to overcome not only a determined and obstinate resistance, but great natural difficulties as well, which had to be overcome before guns could be brought up to support the infantry." 750 prisoners were taken, and 1000 Turkish dead were buried. The fighting 26th–30th December is now designated the " Defence of Jerusalem."

The despatch, paragraph 7, shows that the 60th and 53rd Divisions were engaged in the operations leading to the capture of Jericho, 20th–21st February, 1918.

On 9th, 10th and 11th March further operations were undertaken in which the fighting was of a bitter character. Paragraph 8: On the 9th " the 53rd Division on the right had met with considerable opposition and great natural difficulties especially on the extreme right and at Tell-Asur, a conspicuous landmark among a mass of high hills. The importance attached to it by the enemy was shown by the number of determined efforts he made to recapture

FIFTY-THIRD DIVISION 117

it, all of which were repulsed." Progress continued on the 10th and 11th.

In his third despatch, dated 31st October, Sir E. Allenby describes his final operations, now designated "The Battles of Megiddo," which led to the armistice with Turkey. The main attack was on the coastal plain, that is on the left of the line, the 53rd Division and the 10th Division to make an advance on the right of the line some twelve hours later.

Paragraph 13: "During the night of September 18th–19th the XX. Corps swung forward its right on the east of the Bireh—Nablus road. The 53rd Division descended into the basin at the head of the Wadi Samieh, captured Kh. Jibeit, El Mugheir and the ridge on the far side of the basin and all its objectives with the exception of one hill, Kh. Abu Malul. Considerable opposition was encountered and hand-to-hand fighting took place in which over 400 prisoners were taken."

Paragraph 16: On the morning of the 19th "I ordered the XX. Corps to advance that night on Nablus." The enemy had long expected such an attack and his defences were strong and " the task of the Corps was a difficult one. The enemy in this portion of the field was not disorganised and was able to oppose a stout resistance to the advance. The country is broken and rugged, demanding great physical exertion on the part of the troops and preventing the artillery keeping pace with the infantry. Nevertheless good progress was made on the night of September 19th, and during the following day. The 53rd Division captured Kh. Abu Malul and advanced their line in the centre. On their right Khan Jibeit was heavily counter-attacked on the morning of September 20th. The Turks succeeded in regaining the hill but were driven off again after a sharp fight." By the evening of the 21st the XX. Corps had reached a line which extended to the N.E. of Nablus. After that date the fighting operations were mainly within the sphere of the cavalry and armoured cars, but the infantry had some severe marching and other hardships. On 31st October the Armistice with Turkey came into force.

The Division was unfortunate in losing several of its original units before it went abroad, the 1/4th Royal Welsh Fusiliers, 1/5th and 1/6th Cheshire Regiment and 1/1st, 1/2nd and 1/3rd Monmouth Regiment having been taken to the Western front early in the war. The 1/4th and 1/5th Welsh Regiment, originally Army Troops, the 1/4th Royal Sussex, 2/4th Royal West Surrey, 2/4th Royal West Kent and 2/10th Middlesex took the place of the units which had left the Division. In the despatch of 14th January, 1915, Sir John French gave mention to several officers and men of the 2nd Monmouth Regiment for good work at the First Battle of Ypres, and in his despatch of 31st May, 1915, officers and men of the 1/5th Cheshire and 1/2nd and 1/3rd Monmouth gained mention. The 1/1st Monmouth was Pioneer battalion to the 46th (North Midland) Division and shared its glory on 29th September, 1918, when they crossed the St. Quentin canal, captured Bellenglise and broke the Hindenburg line.

FIFTY-THIRD DIVISION 119

The 1/4th Royal Welsh Fusiliers served as Pioneers to the 47th Division and during the Retreat, March 1918, did outstanding work, particularly on the 24th when acting as rearguard.

The 6th Cheshire is mentioned by Sir A. Conan Doyle, volume iv. p. 146, as in a Territorial brigade of the 39th Division which on 31st July, 1917, in the Third Battle of Ypres, made an attack which was " extraordinarily gallant," " greater constancy has seldom been seen." The same battalion was in the awful fighting on the Aisne at the end of May 1918, when three divisions of the IX. Corps were destroyed. An account of the battle is to be found in the *History of the 25th Division* (Harrison).

As stated under the 52nd, the divisions in Palestine sent battalions to France to reinforce the army there after the losses incurred by it in the great German offensive. The 1/4th Cheshire, 1/1st Hereford and 1/4th Sussex were put into the 34th Division and fought with it in the great battle south of Soissons, July 1918, when Marshal Foch crushed in the sides of the salient between the Aisne and the Marne.

The following units, either belonging to the 53rd Division, or which had served with it, were chosen for the Army of Occupation on the Western Front: 1/4th and 1/6th Cheshire Regiment, 2/4th Royal West Surrey and 1/4th Sussex Regiment. The 1/6th Welsh Regiment, originally Army Troops, was also selected.

54TH (EAST ANGLIAN) DIVISION
First Line

In his despatch of 11th December 1915, dealing with the operations at Suvla Bay, Gallipoli, Sir Ian Hamilton said: " The 54th Division, infantry only, arrived and were disembarked on August 11th and placed in reserve. On the following day, August 12th, I proposed that the 54th Division should make a night-march in order to attack, at dawn on the 13th, the heights Kavak Tepe—Teke Tepe."
" That afternoon the 163rd Brigade moved off and in spite of serious opposition established itself about the A of Anafarta in difficult and enclosed country. In the course of the fight, creditable in all respects to the 163rd Brigade, there happened a very mysterious thing. The 1/5th Norfolks were on the right of the line and found themselves for a moment less strongly opposed than the rest of the brigade. Against the yielding forces of the enemy Colonel Sir H. Beauchamp, a bold, self-confident officer, eagerly pressed forward, followed by the best part of the battalion. The fighting grew hotter, and the ground became more wooded and broken. At this stage many men were wounded or grew exhausted with thirst. These found their way back to camp during the night. But the colonel, with 16 officers and 250 men, still kept pushing on, driving the enemy before him. Amongst

these ardent souls was part of a fine company enlisted from the King's Sandringham estates. Nothing more was ever seen or heard of any of them. They charged into the forest and were lost to sight and sound. Not one of them ever came back."

Owing to representations by the Corps Commander the night march and projected attack on the 13th were abandoned.

The 162nd Brigade of the 54th Division were in support in an attack on 15th August, and on the 21st, the " Battle of Scimitar Hill," " the 53rd and 54th were to hold the enemy from Sulajik to Kiretch Tepe Sirt, while the 29th Division and the 11th Division stormed Ismail Oglu Tepe." These attacks met with little success. During the ensuing four months the Suvla Force held on to the ground it had won, but with ever-increasing difficulty, as sickness and casualties had sadly thinned its ranks.

On the night of the 19th–20th December, 1915, the evacuation from Suvla and Anzac was completed.

The 54th Division sailed for Egypt and down to the close of the war remained part of the Egyptian Expeditionary Force. Shortly after landing in Egypt part of the Division was employed as Lines of Communication troops for the column working on the western frontier. (See Sir J. G. Maxwell's despatch of 1st March, 1916.)

When Sir A. Murray proceeded to press back the Turks in Palestine the 54th Division was employed—quotations from the despatch of 28th June, 1917, as to the action of 26th–27th March,

1917, the "First Battle of Gaza," are given under the 53rd Division.

In the despatch of 28th June, 1917, as to the "Second Battle of Gaza," paragraph 9, Sir A. Murray stated that on 17th April, 1917, the 54th and 52nd "were to seize and occupy the line Sheik-Abbas—Mansura—Kurd Hill," that line was taken by 7 a.m.

On the 19th these two divisions were to attack the Ali Muntar group of works south of Gaza, the 54th pivoting on the right of the 52nd; unfortunately the latter division was held up, see 52nd Division. "Meanwhile the 54th Division with the Imperial Camel Corps had advanced steadily under fire on the right of the 52nd Division. Its left brigade was in advance of the right of the rear brigade of the 52nd Division, and thus exposed to a heavy enfilade fire from the direction of Ali Muntar. At 9.30 a.m. the left of this brigade was heavily counter-attacked, but the enemy were repulsed by machine-gun fire. On the right of this brigade another brigade fought its way forward against the enemy works between Gaza and Khirbet Sihan." These were entered by the Camel Corps. The two brigades, "in spite of most strenuous and gallant efforts to advance, were repeatedly checked by very heavy fire from this front. Towards noon the left of the right brigade was forced back by a determined counter-attack from the north-east," but with the assistance of the third brigade it was able to regain the ground lost.

At 3 p.m.: "Reports received from the 54th Division stated that the situation was satisfactory, and that no help was required to enable the ground gained to be held until further progress by the 52nd should render practicable a renewal of the advance. I should like to state here my appreciation of the great skill with which General Hare handled his fine Division throughout the day." A counter-attack by the Turks at 3.30 p.m. "was shattered." The attack was not pressed further, but the ground gained was consolidated.

Sir E. Allenby took command of the Egyptian Expeditionary Force at the end of June, 1917, and his first despatch, that of 16th December, 1917, shows that in the "Third Battle of Gaza" his main attack on the Gaza—Beersheba line, 27th October–7th November, was from the British right (see 53rd and 60th Divisions), but it was essential to compel the enemy to throw in his reserves at the western end of the line and, to ensure that, the 52nd and 54th Divisions on 2nd and 3rd November assaulted the positions guarding Gaza on the south and west. On the 3rd the 54th after stiff fighting captured several strongly fortified positions, notably the El Arish redoubt, taken by the 1/4th and 1/5th Norfolks, the Rafa redoubt and other posts, taken by the 1/5th and 1/6th Essex, while other battalions of the Division seized the Belah trenches and Turtle Hill. (See Dane's *British Campaigns in the Nearer East*, Hodder and Stoughton, vol. ii. p. 91.) Very heavy counter-attacks to recapture these positions, which were of great importance, were launched by the Turks but these were repulsed with heavy loss to the enemy.

Between the 3rd and 6th the hardest fighting took place east of Gaza, and the enemy's line was

FIFTY-FOURTH DIVISION 125

broken there. The despatch, paragraph 12, notes that " East Anglian troops on the left also found at dawn " (on the 7th) " that the enemy had retired during the night, and early in the morning the main force occupied the northern and eastern defences of Gaza."

The 54th took part in the pursuit and the British advance to the line Jaffa—Jerusalem.

Sir E. Allenby's second despatch, that of 18th September, 1918, shows that the 54th was, along with the 52nd, in the XXI. Corps to which was given the task of increasing the distance between Joppa, or Jaffa, and the enemy. This was duly accomplished on 21st and 22nd December, 1917, in what is now designated the " Battle of Jaffa " (see also 52nd Division). Paragraph 4 of the despatch states that " on the morning of 22nd December, the 54th Division on the right drove the enemy from the orchards which surround Mulebbis and captured the villages of Rantieh and Fejja. On the left the 52nd reached all their objectives."

Paragraph 8 of the despatch shows that early in March the XXI. Corps made a further advance. The 54th captured five villages and some prisoners, and, paragraph 16, the Corps again moved forward, 9th to 11th April, when other positions were taken and held against the heavy counter-attacks in which the enemy's losses were considerable, " over 300 of his dead being counted "

In his last despatch, that of 31st October, 1918, Sir E. Allenby described how his infantry broke through the Turkish lines and opened the gate for the cavalry and armoured cars.

126 THE TERRITORIAL DIVISIONS

Paragraph 15: "The attack on the coastal plain on the morning of September 19th was attended with complete success. On the right, in the foothills, the French Tirailleurs and the Armenians of the Légion d'Orient advanced with great dash." "On their left the 54th Division stormed Kefr Kasim village and wood and the foothills overlooking the railway from Ras El Ain to Jiljulieh. North of Kefr Kasim the advance was checked for a time at Sivri Tepe, but the enemy's resistance was quickly overcome and the remaining hills south of the Wadi Kanah captured." "The 3rd, Lahore, Division pressed on eastwards into the foothills, near Hableh, joining hands with the 54th Division north of the Wadi Kanah." Later the 7th, Meerut, 3rd, Lahore, and 54th Divisions advanced further in an easterly direction.

After this the infantry of the XXI. Corps were never seriously opposed but they had many most severe marches during the next three weeks.

Like its neighbour in the East, the 53rd, the 54th Division lost some good battalions before it went abroad as a division. The policy pursued in 1914 and first half of 1915 of "picking the eyes out of" Territorial divisions has been severely animadverted upon, by, among others, Sir Ian Hamilton, and no one was better qualified than he was to judge of the wisdom or folly of this proceeding.

The 1st Hertfordshire Regiment, the 1st Cambridgeshire Regiment and the 4th Suffolk Regiment, originally units of the 54th Division, went early to France. The Hertfordshire battalion was mentioned in Sir John French's despatch of 20th

FIFTY-FOURTH DIVISION 127

November, 1914, as among the territorial battalions which took part in the First Battle of Ypres (see 56th Division). The despatch of 2nd February 1915, paragragh 4, shows that the 4th Suffolk Regiment was part of a force making a counter-attack near Givenchy on 20th December, 1914. " About 5 p.m. a gallant attack by the 1st Manchester Regiment and one company 4th Suffolk Regiment had captured Givenchy, and had cleared the enemy out of two lines of trenches to the north-east."

In the despatch of 15th June, 1915, as to the Second Battle of Ypres, 22nd April to 25th May, the great gas attack, the Commander-in-Chief, quoting Sir Herbert Plumer, gives some examples of " individual gallantry," among these he mentions the visit by a patrol, two officers and one N.C.O. of the 1st Cambridgeshire to a German trench, 350 yards away. The adventurous party, with great good fortune, got safely back to their own trench. Officers and men of these units were mentioned by Sir John French.

The places of these three battalions in the 54th Division were taken by the 1/10th and 1/11th County of London Regiment from the 56th Division and the 1/8th Hampshire, a Wessex battalion.

Sir A. Conan Doyle, volume iv. p. 198, draws attention to the fine work of the 33rd Division in the Third Battle of Ypres on 26th September, 1917, and among other battalions highly spoken of is the 4th Suffolks. In the same volume, p. 146, he refers to the 1st Hertfordshire and 1st Cambridgeshire, then both in the 39th Division, in terms of praise, for their conduct in the same battle on 31st July.

128 THE TERRITORIAL DIVISIONS

In volume v. p. 117, he mentions the 1st Hertfordshire, 39th Division, as retaking "in very gallant fashion," on 22nd March, 1918, a village which had been lost, and says the battalion had greatly distinguished itself at St. Julien and elsewhere. In volume vi. he refers to the gallantry and steadiness of that battalion in connection with the action about Trescault, 18th September, 1918, and in the same volume, pp. 33, 62 and 287, he gives great credit to the 1st Cambridgeshire for fine conduct on three occasions in 1918, when serving with the 12th Division.

These words of praise mean much, as throughout the work individual battalions are not often mentioned.

The following units which had either belonged originally to the 54th or had fought with it were chosen for the Armies of Occupation: The Rhine, 1/4th Suffolk Regiment; Egypt and Palestine, 1/4th Norfolk Regiment, 1/5th Suffolk Regiment, 1/4th, 1/5th and 1/7th Essex Regiment, 1/4th Northamptonshire Regiment and 1/10th London Regiment.

55TH (WEST LANCASHIRE) DIVISION
FIRST LINE

As in the case of some other good divisions, the 55th, as a unit, suffered because its individual battalions were early ready and eager to go to France. Had it been otherwise the history of the Division would have been at least one year longer. The 10th Liverpool Regiment went to France in October 1914, and the other battalions followed during the succeeding six months. For the most part the battalions were, on landing, attached to Regular brigades. The 5th Royal Lancaster, 5th, 7th and 9th Liverpool, and 5th South Lancashire all bore a conspicuous part in the Second Battle of Ypres, now "The Battles of Ypres, 1915," the gas attack, April and May 1915, and nobly helped to stem the German flood; or in the battles of Richebourg-St.-Vaast — Festubert, 9th–16th May, 1915. The North Lancashire Brigade was attached to the 51st, Highland, Division and played a prominent part in that division's first battle on 15th–16th June. The 4th Loyal North Lancashire, 4th Royal Lancaster and 8th Liverpool all fought with distinction in that engagement and suffered very heavy losses. On the same day, 16th June, the 10th Liverpool, now a band of veteran soldiers, was employed with the 3rd Division in an attack at Hooge and made a fine, almost over-eager, advance. Their losses are said by Sir A. Conan Doyle to have exceeded 400. The Division was represented in the Loos battle, September 1915, by the 9th Liverpool.

In Sir John French's despatch of 14th January, 1915, giving the names of those who had distinguished themselves prior to the end of November 1914, he mentions an officer and N.C.O. of the 10th Liverpool, and in that of 31st May, 1915, officers and men of the 5th Royal Lancaster, 10th Liverpool, 4th South Lancashire and 5th Loyal North Lancashire. Subsequently other names were mentioned for the Ypres battle and for the battles about Festubert.

The individual battalions were brought together, and the Division reconstituted as a unit, under Major-General H. S. Jeudwine, in January 1916. By that date several battalions had few of their original members on their strength.

In February the Division joined the XIV. Corps south of Arras. At the end of July they were taken to the Somme. On 30th July the Division entered the line under the XIV. Corps opposite Guillemont on the extreme right of the British Army, the French being their neighbours on the right flank. On 8th, 9th and 12th August the Division attacked and a certain amount of ground was gained and consolidated, but the village was not taken. From 16th August to 4th September they were at rest and then entered the line under the XV. Corps near Delville Wood. They took part in an attack on 9th September, the "Battle of Ginchy."

The despatch from Sir Douglas Haig of 23rd December, 1916, deals with the Somme battle. Para-

FIFTY-FIFTH DIVISION 131

graph 29 (Dent's edition), shows that the 55th was employed in the big attack by the Fourth Army beginning on 25th September, now designated the "Battle of Morval." The objectives "included a belt of country about 1000 yards deep, curving round the north of Flers to a point midway between that village and Martinpuich (55th Division, Major-General H. S. Jeudwine, and New Zealand and 1st Divisions)." These objectives were gained.

Paragraph 31 states: "On the Fourth Army front on 27th September a further portion of the enemy's fourth system of defence north-west of Gueudecourt was carried on a front of a mile by the 55th and New Zealand Divisions." A further "very considerable advance," was made in the afternoon and evening.

On the night of the 28th September, the Division left the line and was ordered to the Ypres salient. The Commander of the Fourth Army sent them a message which spoke of their good work and their "spirit of gallantry and endurance."

The Division was still in the salient when the great attack of 31st July, 1917, took place. That assault was the beginning of the Third Battle of Ypres, now "The Battles of Ypres, 1917."

Sir Douglas Haig's despatch of 25th December, 1917, paragraph 41 (Dent's edition), deals with the initial assault launched at 3.50 a.m. on 31st July, and states: "At 9 a.m. the whole of our second objectives north of the Ypres—Roulers railway were in our possession with the exception of a strong point north of Frezenberg, known as Pommern Redoubt, where fighting was still going on. Within an hour

132 THE TERRITORIAL DIVISIONS

this redoubt had also been captured by West Lancashire Territorials (55th Division)." In this attack the Division was in the XIX. Corps, Fifth Army. See note, Messrs. Dent's edition, p. 113. The operations 31st July–2nd August are now designated the "Battle of Pilckem Ridge."

Paragraph 50 of the same despatch gives an account of the attack launched at 5.40 a.m. on 20th September (the Battle of the Menin Road Ridge), "a most successful operation," notwithstanding the excessively bad state of the ground. "West Lancashire Territorials (55th Division) found the ground south-east of St. Julien very wet and heavy after the night's rain. None the less, they made steady progress, reaching the line of their final objectives early in the afternoon."

Needless to say, the losses of the Division in the Third Battle of Ypres were heavy.

In the last week of September the Division left the salient after over eleven months' service there. They were taken to the Epéhy district south-west of Cambrai and at once entered the line.

The Division held the right of the battle line when the British attacked on 20th November, 1917 (the "Battle of Cambrai, 1917"). In his telegraphic despatch of 21st November, Sir Douglas Haig said: "West Lancashire Territorials broke through positions about Epéhy." This part of the attack was really a feint or holding attack, but it cost the Division heavy casualties.

On 30th November the enemy made his great counter-attack with very strong forces. The Division held the southern part of the British line where it was attacked. The Divisional frontage was nearly eight miles, and as it was impossible to man a continuous line, it was held by posts. Another British division was on the right of the 55th but it was not seriously involved in the fighting on 20th and 30th November.

The battle is described in paragraphs 9 and 10 of the despatch of 20th February, 1918.

Paragraph 9 states: " From the Banteux ravine southwards the divisions in line were weak and held very extended fronts." " In view of the symptoms of activity observed on the enemy's front, special precautions were taken by local commanders, especially from Villers Guislain to the south." The map opposite p. 163 of Messrs. Dent's edition shows the latter portion to have been in the area of the 55th Division.

Paragraph 10: " Between the hours of 7 and 8 a.m. on the last day of November, the enemy attacked, after a short but intense artillery preparation, on the greater part of a front of some ten miles, from Vendhuille " (on our right) " to Masnières " (on our left) " inclusive. From Masnières to Banteux, both inclusive, four German divisions would seem to have been employed against the three British divisions holding this area (29th, 20th and 12th)." The map above referred to shows these are from left to right. " Between Banteux exclusive and Vendhuille one German division and portions of two others were employed against the northern half of the British division holding that front (the 55th Division, Major-General H. S. Jeudwine)."

" At the northern end of the Bonavis Ridge,

and in the Gonnelieu sector [1] the swiftness with which the advance of the enemy's infantry followed the opening of his bombardment appears to have overwhelmed our troops, both in line and in immediate support, almost before they had realised that the attack had begun."

"East of Villers Guislain [2] the troops holding our forward positions on the high ground were still offering a strenuous resistance to the enemy's attack on their front, at a time when large forces of German infantry had already advanced up the valley between them and Villers Guislain. South of this village a single strong point known as Limerick Post, garrisoned by troops of the 1/5th Battalion (King's Own), Royal Lancaster Regiment and the 1/10th Battalion, Liverpool Regiment (both of the 55th Division), held out with great gallantry throughout the day, although heavily attacked.

"The progress made by the enemy, however, across the northern end of the Bonavis Ridge and up the deep gully between Villers Guislain and Gonnelieu, known as 22 Ravine, turned our positions on the ridge as well as in both villages."

Towards the close of the despatch, paragraph 15, Sir Douglas Haig said: "On the 30th November risks were accepted by us at some points in order to increase our strength at others. Our fresh reserves had been thrown in on the Bourlon front, where the enemy brought against us a total force of seven divisions to three and failed. I do not

---
[1] The Bonavis Ridge is north-west and Gonnelieu is west of Banteux.
[2] This appears to have been in the area of the 55th Division.

consider it would have been justifiable on the indications to have allotted a smaller garrison to this front." And again: " Though the defence broke down for a time in one area the recovery made by the weak forces still left and those within reach is worthy of the highest praise. Numberless instances of great gallantry, promptitude and skill were shown, some few of which have been recounted."

It would be against the spirit of what has been said in the introduction if any stress were laid here on what a unit said about itself, but in view of the discussion which took place on the events of 30th November it does seem fair to say that in the *Story of the 55th Division* (*Liverpool Daily Post* Office), there is quoted a letter from the Commander of the VII. Corps, under which the Division was serving on the 30th, in which he said: " He knows that the 30th November, 1917, in spite of the heavy losses incurred, was a day which will always reflect credit on the 55th Division. The fact that not a man returned from the 5th South Lancashire Regiment " (the battalion next the ravine) " when that battalion was attacked by overwhelming numbers, tells its own tale." In a message on another occasion he said: " It cannot be contradicted by anyone that the 55th saved the day on November 30th, 1917. You got a most infernal hammering, but you saved the day."

On 8th December the Division was relieved and shortly afterwards moved north. After two months' training, when much-needed drafts were absorbed, the Division entered the line in the Givenchy—Festubert area on 15th February, 1918. About this time brigades were reduced from four to three battalions. The 1/8th and 1/9th Liverpool Regiment and 1/5th Loyal North Lancashire were taken out of the 55th and sent to the 57th. In the beginning of 1918 there was difficulty in keeping second line divisions up to establishment.

When the Lys battle broke out the 55th Division was put to as severe a test as could be imagined, and stood it magnificently. The Division was congratulated in an order by the Commander-in-Chief, and the terms of his supplementary despatch, dated 15th April, 1918, could not have been more flattering. It was as follows:

"The 55th Division at Givenchy, 9th–14th April, 1918.
Headquarters, France, Monday, 1.15 p.m.

"On the morning of the German attack on the 9th April, 1918, the 55th (West Lancashire) Division (Territorial) was holding a front of about 6000 yards, extending from the La Bassée Canal to just south of Richebourg l'Avoué, where its line joined that held by the Portuguese.

"The enemy's attack on the southern portion of this front was delivered by all three regiments of the 4th Ersatz Division, which was well up to strength.

"A captured Divisional order issued by the General Staff of this German Division, and dated 6th April, 1918, shows that its objectives were 'the ground and the British position in the triangle formed by Givenchy—Festubert—Gorre.'

"The following passages from this captured order are of special interest.

FIFTY-FIFTH DIVISION 137

"'In our attack our three regiments will be opposed by at most six companies in front and at most two reserve battalions in Festubert and Givenchy. One battalion in divisional reserve is south of the La Bassée Canal, in Le Preol. It will be prevented by our powerful artillery fire from taking part in the fight for Festubert and Givenchy. The troops are elements of the English 55th Division, which, after being engaged on the Somme, has suffered heavy losses in Flanders and at Cambrai, and was described by prisoners in March, 1918, as a division fit to hold a quiet sector, that is below the average quality.'

"The order containing the passages quoted above was distributed among all officers and under-officers of the 4th Ersatz Division down to platoon-commanders, presumably with a view to encouraging the troops prior to their attack, and in the belief that the opposition met with would not be very serious. If this was his expectation, the enemy was most signally disappointed.

"Throughout the early part of the morning of the 9th April, the 55th Division beat off all attacks in its forward zone, and maintained its line intact.

"Later, when the German infantry had broken through the Portuguese positions on its left, the Division formed a defensive flank facing north-east on the line Givenchy—Festubert to the neighbourhood of Le Touret. This line it maintained practically unchanged until relief, through six days of almost continual fighting, in the course of which it beat off repeated German attacks with the heaviest losses to the enemy, and took nearly a thousand prisoners.

"At one time, on the first day of his attack, the enemy's troops forced their way into Givenchy and Festubert. Both villages were shortly afterwards regained by the 55th Division as the result of a highly successful counter-attack, in which several hundred Germans were captured.

"All further attempts on the part of the enemy to carry these positions broke down before the resolute defence of the 55th Division. Though he succeeded on the 11th April in entering a post north of Festubert, he was thrown out again by a counter-attack, and on the night of the 12th April the 55th Division improved its position in this neighbourhood, capturing a German post and taking several prisoners.

"Next day, during the afternoon, the enemy heavily bombarded the whole front held by the Division between Gorre and the Lawe Canal, and subsequently attacked in strength. He was once more repulsed with heavy loss by the most gallant and successful defence of a division which he had been pleased to describe as consisting of second-class troops."

The fine conduct of the Division was again referred to in the despatch of 20th July, 1918, which deals with the Lys battle, paragraph 51. It was there stated that "Throughout the remainder of the day, 9th April, the 55th Division maintained its positions against all assaults, and by successful counter-attacks captured over 750 prisoners. The success of this most gallant defence, the importance of which it would be hard to over-estimate, was due in great measure to the courage and determination displayed by our advance posts. These held out with the utmost resolution though surrounded, pinning to the ground those parties of the enemy who had penetrated our defences, and preventing them from developing their attack. Among the many gallant deeds recorded of them, one instance is known of a machine gun which was kept in action although the German infantry had entered the rear compartment of the 'pill-box' from which it was firing, the gun team holding up the enemy by revolver fire from the inner compartment."

The losses of the Division at Givenchy exceeded 3000.

The despatch of 21st December, 1918, paragraph 40, shows that in September there was sharp fighting in which the 16th, 55th and 19th Divisions pressed back the enemy and "advanced our line close to the outskirts of La Bassée."

During the remainder of September pressure was kept up by the I. Corps, now in the Fifth Army, including the 55th Division. In October the enemy withdrew slowly, and the Division followed closely on his heels, driving in rearguards and at times meeting with very stubborn opposition. On 8th October the III. Corps took control and the same policy was pursued. The Haute Deule canal was crossed on the night of 15th–16th October after a good deal of fighting. On the morning of 11th November the town of Ath was occupied.

An excellent account of the work of the Division will be found in *The Story of the 55th (West*

Lancashire) Division, by the Rev. J. O. Coop, D.S.O., T.D., Liverpool, 1919.

The 1/5th Royal Lancaster Regiment, 1/10th Liverpool Regiment, and 1/5th South Lancashire Regiment were chosen for the Armies of Occupation.

56TH (LONDON) DIVISION, FORMERLY 1ST LONDON. FIRST LINE

THE 56th Division does not seem to have been mentioned as a unit till 1916; the reason was that its individual battalions went to France early in the war, being attached to Regular divisions and, as in the case of the 55th, many months elapsed before the Division was concentrated.

Unofficial historians over and over again refer to the splendid service performed by battalions of the 56th during the critical first winter of the war, and in the second awful struggle at Ypres in April and May 1915. Before the Division was constituted as a unit in France many of these battalions had few of their original members left. Sir A. Conan Doyle mentions that on 12th May, 1915, before the close of the battle, the 5th London had only 200 men.

In Sir John French's despatch of 20th November, 1914, dealing with the First Battle of Ypres, 11th October to 12th November, he said, paragraph 10: " In the period covered by this despatch Territorial troops have been used for the first time in the Army under my command," and he mentioned "the London Scottish and Queen's Westminster battalions" as among the units actually engaged; both were afterwards in the 56th Division. " The conduct and bearing of these units under fire, and the efficient manner in which they carried out the various duties assigned to them, have imbued me with the highest

142 THE TERRITORIAL DIVISIONS

hope as to the value and help of Territorial troops generally." Events were to prove these hopes well-founded.

Officers and men of the 5th City of London Regiment and of the 9th, 13th and 14th County of London Regiment were mentioned in the despatch of 14th January, 1915, for good work in the fighting before that date, and in the despatch of 31st May, 1915, many officers and men of the 3rd, 4th and 5th City of London and of the 9th, 12th, 13th, 14th and 16th County of London, gained mention; all these battalions were afterwards in the 56th Division.

In Sir John French's despatch of 15th June, 1915, paragraph 4, regarding " The Battles of Ypres, 1915," which commenced on the 22nd April of that year with the great "gas attack," he mentioned two battalions of the 56th Division. As to the fighting on 8th May, quoting Sir Herbert Plumer, " A counter-attack was launched at 3.30 p.m." " The 12th London Regiment, on the left, succeeded, at great cost, in reaching the original trench line, and did considerable execution with their machine gun." As to the 13th May, when another serious German attack was made "after the heaviest bombardment yet experienced, . . . the 5th London Regiment, despite very heavy casualties, maintained their position unfalteringly."

The Division, like other first line Territorial divisions, had their full share of fighting in the big battles of 1916 and 1917.

Sir Douglas Haig's despatch of 23rd December, 1916, paragraph 8 (Dent's edition), shows that the 56th along with the 46th Division made the sub-

FIFTY-SIXTH DIVISION 143

sidiary attack at Gommecourt, north of the Somme, on 1st July. They were then in the Third Army, VII. Corps. (See 46th Division.)

The 56th was afterwards sent to the XIV. Corps, Fourth Army, and took part in the successful attack of 9th September, now officially the " Battle of Ginchy." Paragraph 23: " At Ginchy and to the north of Leuze Wood it met with almost immediate success. On the right (56th Division) the enemy's line was seized over a front of more than 1000 yards." Paragraphs 27 and 28 deal with another successful attack on 15th September and following days, officially the " Battle of Flers-Courcelette," when the Division was again employed.

While the French worked up the south side of Combles, the 56th encompassed it from the north and, on 26th September, met their Allies in the town. Down to the close of the Somme battles, the Division, " hard-worked and splendid," Sir A. Conan Doyle describes them, " were doing fine work always on the extreme right."

The fighting between 25th and 28th September has been designated the " Battle of Morval," and that between 1st and 18th October, the " Battle of the Transloy Ridges."

The despatch of 25th December, 1917, paragraph 13 (Dent's edition), shows that the 56th, again in the VII. Corps, Third Army, took part in the Battle of Arras which opened on 9th April, 1917. Paragraph 14: " By 12 noon the 12th Division had captured Observation Ridge and, with the exception of Railway Triangle, the whole of our second objectives were in our possession from south of

144 THE TERRITORIAL DIVISIONS

Neuville Vitasse, stormed by London Territorials (56th Division), to north of La Folie Farm." A large number of prisoners were taken. The 56th had an extremely difficult task and met with stubborn resistance. As was to be expected, their losses were considerable.

Paragraph 17: " On 12th April our attacks on Héninel and Wancourt were renewed, and our troops (21st and 56th Divisions) succeeded in carrying both villages, as well as in completing the capture of the Hindenburg line for some 2000 yards south of the Cojeul river."

Paragraph 27: On 11th May " London troops (56th Division) captured Cavalry Farm."

In addition to the actions mentioned in these extracts, the Division was engaged throughout the Arras operations on many other occasions, notably on 13th and 14th April and on 3rd May, when one brigade made an excellent advance. Throughout the battles of Arras the work of the 56th was of outstanding merit.

The fighting between 9th and 14th April is now the " First Battle of the Scarpe, 1917," and that on 3rd and 4th May the " Third Battle of the Scarpe, 1917."

The Division was employed on 16th August, 1917, in the second big attack in the Third Battle of Ypres, now " The Battles of Ypres, 1917." The action of 16th August is now designated the " Battle of Langemarck."

Paragraph 46 of the same despatch: " On the right of the British attack the enemy again developed the main strength of his resistance. At the end of a day of very heavy fighting, except for small gains of ground on the western edge of Glencorse Wood and north of Westhoek by the 56th Division (Major-General F. A. Dudgeon) and the 8th Division the situation south of St. Julien remained unchanged."

The losses of the Division on the 16th August were extremely heavy. In the Ypres battle they were in the II. Corps.

When the Cambrai battle commenced on 20th November the 56th were not in the main assault on the 20th but kept up a feint or subsidiary attack on that date.

In the despatch of Sir Douglas Haig, dated 20th February, 1918, as to the " Battle of Cambrai, 1917," paragraph 6, he said that the 22nd November 1917 was spent in organising the ground which had been captured on the 20th and 21st, carrying out reliefs, etc. " Meanwhile, early in the night of the 22nd November, a battalion of the Queen's Westminsters (16th London), 56th Division, Major-General F. A. Dudgeon, stormed a commanding tactical point in the Hindenburg line, west of Mœuvres, known as Tadpole Copse, the possession of which would be of value in connection with the left flank of the Bourlon position when the latter had been secured."

Paragraph 7 deals with the renewal of the British attack on 23rd November. " Throughout this day also the 36th Division and troops of the 56th (London) Division (T.) were engaged in stubborn fighting in the neighbourhood of Mœuvres and Tadpole Copse and made some progress."

On the 27th there was again heavy fighting.

146 THE TERRITORIAL DIVISIONS

"During the afternoon the enemy also attacked our positions at Tadpole Copse but was repulsed."

Paragraphs 10-11 deal with the great German counter-attack of 30th November, and a quotation in which the 47th and 56th Divisions are both said to have greatly distinguished themselves, is given under the former. The fine conduct of both divisions could not have been surpassed.

In Sir Douglas Haig's despatch of 20th July, 1918, he gives a detailed account of the German attack in the Cambrai—St. Quentin district which commenced on 21st March, and compelled the retreat of the Fifth Army, and the partial withdrawal of the Third.

At paragraph 45 he describes the attack on the Arras front, an extension to the north of the earlier attacks. "Meanwhile, between 7 and 8 a.m. on the morning of March 28th, fighting of the utmost intensity had broken out north of the Somme from Puisieux to north-east of Arras. Finding himself checked on the northern flank of his attack the enemy on this day made a determined effort to obtain greater freedom for the development of his offensive, and struck in great force along the valley of the Scarpe at Arras." . . . "After a bombardment of great violence, three fresh German divisions advanced to the assault along the north bank of the Scarpe river against the positions held by the 4th and 56th British Divisions under the command respectively of Major-General T. G. Matheson and Major-General F. A. Dudgeon, and were supported in their attack by the two German divisions already in line." . . . "His troops were everywhere stopped and thrown back with the heaviest loss before our battle positions." "A second attack late in the afternoon north of the Scarpe, after a further period of bombardment, was also repulsed at all points. At the end of the day our battle positions astride the Scarpe were intact on the whole front of the attack, and in the evening successful counter-attacks enabled us to push out a new outpost line in front of them. Meanwhile the surviving garrisons of our original outpost line, whose most gallant resistance had played so large a part in breaking up the enemy's attack, had fought their way back through the enemy."

His defeat on the 28th weakened the enemy's offensive and it eventually closed a few days later. The stand made by the Division, on the flank of the attack, where it was strongly pressed, was not excelled by the performance of any other unit during the March battle, and greatly contributed to the cessation of the German effort. The fighting on 28th March is now the "First Battle of Arras, 1918." The Division was at that time in the XIII. Corps, First Army (see paragraph 45 of the despatch). It was the only division of the First Army engaged on the 28th.

In his telegraphic despatch of 13th September, 1918, as to the good work of various divisions in the early days of the last British offensive, under the heading 56th Division, Sir Douglas Haig said: "The 56th Division, which on March 28th assisted in the repulse of the German attack north of the Scarpe, on August 23rd attacked successfully, with the 52nd Division, at Boyelles and Hénin-sur-

148 THE TERRITORIAL DIVISIONS

Cojeul. These two divisions met with very vigorous resistance about Croisilles and the important feature known as Hénin Hill to the north of it, but captured both places. On August 29th by a daring operation the h56t Division and the 57th Division captured Bullecourt and Hendicourt - lez - Cagnicourt. The possession of both villages was fiercely disputed, but on September 1st the 52nd and 57th Divisions secured firm hold of them and took Riencourt-lez-Cagnicourt. Also on September 2nd the 52nd and 57th Divisions continued the attack, with the 63rd Division, and captured Quéant, Pronville and Fontaine-lez-Croisilles."

The despatch of 21st December, 1918, shows that the 56th Division was on 23rd August in the VI. Corps, Third Army. These events are again referred to in paragraphs 22, 23 and 28.

Paragraph 22 as to 24th August states: " On the left troops of the 56th Division, Major-General Sir C. P. A. Hull, had heavy fighting about Croisilles and on the high ground north-west of that village known as Hénin Hill."

About 25th August the XVII. Corps was formed with the 52nd, 56th, and 57th Divisions, and later the 63rd. In the beginning of September the 56th became part of the XXII. Corps, First Army. Sir Arthur Conan Doyle, vol. vi. p. 133, puts the losses of the Division between 27th and 31st August at 2723 and the prisoners they took at over 1000.

In paragraph 23 as to 29th August, Sir Douglas Haig said: " To the north of Bapaume a gallant thrust by the 56th and 57th Divisions penetrated

FIFTY-SIXTH DIVISION 149

the enemy's position as far as Riencourt - lez - Cagnicourt."

Paragraph 35: "The Battle of Cambrai and the Hindenburg Line, 27th September–5th October," states: "On the extreme left the 56th Division of the XXII. Corps" (on 27th September) crossed the canal and, having cleared Sauchy Lestrée and Sauchy Cauchy, moved northwards to Palluel."

About 11th and 12th October the Division was employed in attacks; it took Fresnes and moved forward, overcoming various obstacles.

The various actions between August and October are now officially defined as follows: 21st–23rd August, the Battle of Albert, 1918; 26th–30th August, Battle of the Scarpe, 1918; 2nd–3rd September, Battle of the Drocourt—Quéant Line; 27th September–1st October, Battle of the Canal du Nord; 8th–12th October, Battle of Cambrai, 1918, with Pursuit to Selle.

Paragraph 50 describes "The Battle of the Sambre, 1st–11th November." Regarding the 4th–6th November: "On the front of the First Army, the XXII. Corps and the Canadian Corps advanced against little opposition except on their right. Here the 11th and 56th Divisions, having crossed the Aunelle river and captured the villages of Le Triez, Sebourg and Sebourg Quiaux, were counter-attacked on the high ground east of the Aunelle and pressed back slightly."

On the 6th the Division after heavy fighting gained its objectives. The advance continued between 7th November and the 11th, Armistice Day.

It will have been observed that all references

150 THE TERRITORIAL DIVISIONS

to the work of the Division were invariably of a laudatory character.

The 1/10th and 1/11th County of London Regiment, originally belonging to the 56th, served with the 54th (East Anglian) Division at Suvla Bay, Gallipoli, and in Palestine, their places being taken by the 1/7th and 1/8th Middlesex from the 44th (Home Counties) Division.

The 1/6th City of London Regiment, originally belonging to the 56th, but which served with the 47th, the 1/9th County of London Regiment of the 56th and the 1/7th Middlesex, which belonged to the 44th, but served with the 56th, were selected for the Army of the Rhine. The 1/10th County of London Regiment, which, as above stated, served with the 54th, was chosen for the Army of Occupation, Egypt.

57TH (WEST LANCASHIRE) DIVISION

SECOND LINE

THE Division went to France in February, 1917, and was employed in the Bailleul—Armentières—Ypres area during the greater part of 1917, and for the first four months of 1918.

A quotation, in which West Lancashire Territorials are mentioned as taking part in an advance in " The Battles of Ypres, 1917," on 16th August, 1917, has been given under the 48th Division. The number of the West Lancashire Division is not given in the *Gazette* or in Messrs. Dent's edition of *Sir Douglas Haig's Despatches*. It seems to be the case that the infantry of the 55th or 57th was not present on that date. The reference may apply to some West Lancashire Artillery.

The 57th did attack as part of the XIV. Corps on 26th October, the " Second Battle of Passchendaele," see 50th Division. Ground was gained, but the conditions were most difficult and the casualties of the 57th were very heavy.

Early in May 1918 the 57th took over from the 42nd in the Bucquoy area, south of Arras.

In August one brigade of the 57th was, for a time, attached to the 51st Division on the Scarpe and took part in a preliminary attack on the 19th. During that month the XVII. Corps, which embraced the 52nd, 56th, 57th, and later the 63rd

152 THE TERRITORIAL DIVISIONS

Divisions, took over in that area, coming in between the VI. Corps and the Canadians.

The XVII. Corps, as part of the Third Army, attacked on the 25th August (see 52nd and 56th), and the 57th entered the front line on the night of the 27th. It had very severe fighting between 28th August and 2nd September and did well, as appears from the extracts referred to below.

In the telegraphic despatch of 13th September, 1918, as to the work of certain divisions, a quotation from which has already been given under the 56th, the 57th was mentioned for its fine services about Bullecourt and there is also given under the 56th a quotation from the despatch of 21st December, 1918, paragraph 23, which applies to both divisions.

Paragraph 28 of the latter despatch deals with the storming of the Drocourt — Quéant line, 2nd September, 1918. " This gallant feat of arms was carried out by," among other troops, " the XVII. Corps of the Third Army employing the 52nd, 57th, and 63rd Divisions." A quotation as to the battle on that date has been given under the 52nd. In the afternoon there was hard fighting but the enemy's opposition was overcome by nightfall " and the 57th Division, swinging to the right, was threatening the villages of Quéant and Pronville from the north." During the night and following day the enemy rapidly retreated.

The fighting in the area in which the XVII. Corps was then operating, 26th-30th August, is now the " Battle of the Scarpe, 1918," and that on 2nd-3rd September, the " Battle of the Drocourt —Quéant Line."

FIFTY-SEVENTH DIVISION 153

In the big and fiercely contested battle commencing on 27th September the XVII. Corps had again to make an effort almost, if not quite, as great as that which broke the Quéant line on 2nd September, and nothing could have been finer than the work of the 52nd, 57th, and 63rd Divisions on this second occasion. The position of the enemy was of immense strength and a wide and deep canal was among the obstacles to be overcome in the advance of the Corps. The fighting on the front of the XVII. Corps lasted, almost without intermission, from 27th September to 1st October. This is now designated the " Battle of the Canal du Nord."

Paragraph 35 of the despatch of 21st December, 1918, dealing with " the Battle of Cambrai and the Hindenburg Line, 27th September–5th October," states: " In the centre the 52nd Division passing its troops across the canal by bridgeheads previously established by the 57th Division, on the opening of the assault carried the German lines east of the canal," etc., but in Messrs. Dent's edition, p. 281, there is the following note: " This is incorrect. There were no bridgeheads at this time and the crossings were forced by the 52nd Division at the opening of their attack."

The despatch proceeds: " As soon as the line of the canal had been secured our engineer troops commenced the construction of bridges, completing their task with remarkable speed, and working with great gallantry under the fire of the German guns. Greatly assisted by their efforts our advance continued. Obstinate resistance was met with at Graincourt, and it was not until late in the day that the village was finally surrounded and captured by the 63rd Division. The 57th Division (Major-General R. W. R. Barnes) meanwhile had passed through and carried the line forward east of Anneux to Fontaine-Notre-Dame."

In paragraph 42, "The Second Battle of Le Cateau, 8th – 12th October," now officially designated the "Battle of Cambrai, 1918," the despatch shows that on 8th October the Third and Fourth Armies attacked and very heavy fighting ensued. "On the extreme left the 57th Division made progress in the southern outskirts of Cambrai. . . . During the following night the Canadian Corps captured Ramillies and crossed the Scheldt canal at Pont d'Aire. Canadian patrols entered Cambrai from the north and joined hands with patrols of the 57th Division working through the southern portion of the town." Next day, "Cambrai was in our hands and our troops were three miles to the east of the town." Progress continued on the 10th. Shortly after this the 57th was taken out of the XVII. Corps and entered the XI. Corps, Fifth Army.

The operations referred to above turned the defences of Lille from the south, and paragraph 45, dealing with "The Evacuation of Lille," states that the 57th and 59th Divisions were by the evening of 17th October "on the outskirts of Lille." These divisions were then in the XI. Corps.

Thereafter the work of the 57th Division was less arduous; the fighting in the area of the Fifth Army was not so severe as it had been on the fronts of the Third and Fourth Armies farther south.

58TH (1ST LONDON) DIVISION

SECOND LINE

THE Division went to France in January 1917. In March and April 1917, Gough's Fifth Army, which contained the 7th, 58th and 62nd Divisions and Australians, was pressing the enemy towards the Hindenburg line, south of Bullecourt. In April as that line was approached the resistance became stronger. While the Arras battle was proceeding on the left (see 56th Division) the Fifth Army had some severe struggles, in the course of which the line at Bullecourt was pierced. In these actions the Australians did splendid work and they were nobly backed up by the three British divisions.

Sir Douglas Haig's despatch of 25th December, 1917, paragraph 27 (Dent's edition), shows that on 7th May, 1917, towards the close of the Arras battle, the 7th Division "gained a footing in the south-east corner of Bullecourt. Thereafter gradual progress was made in face of the most obstinate resistance and on the 17th May, London and West Riding Territorials (58th and 62nd Divisions) completed the capture of the village." The Division remained in the southern area for some months. On 8th July it took over from the 42nd in the Havrincourt sector.

The Division was employed in the Third Battle of Ypres as part of the XVIII. Corps, which it joined early in August.

Paragraph 50 of the same despatch deals with

the "most successful" assault which was launched during that battle on 20th September, 1917. "North of the Zonnebeke—Langemarck road London and Highland Territorials (58th and 51st Divisions) gained the whole of their objectives by midday, though stiff fighting took place for a number of farms and strong places." The official designation of this action is now the "Battle of Menin Road Ridge."

Paragraph 52, as to the attack on 26th September: "The assault was delivered at 5.50 a.m. and, after hard and prolonged fighting in which over 1600 prisoners were taken by us, achieved a success as striking as that of the 20th September." Australian troops carried the remainder of Polygon Wood, etc., on their left the 3rd Division took Zonnebeke. "North Midland and London Territorial battalions (59th Division, Major-General C. F. Romer, and 58th Division) captured a long line of hostile strong points on both sides of the Wieltje—Gravenstafel road." This is now the "Battle of Polygon Wood."

Paragraph 59, as to the assault on the Passchendaele Ridge on 26th October, the "Second Battle of Passchendaele": "On the left of the Canadians the Royal Naval Division and battalions of London Territorials (58th Division, Major-General A. B. E. Cator) also advanced and, in spite of immense difficulties from marsh and floods in the more low-lying ground, made progress."

Paragraph 60, as to the attack on 30th October when the Canadians continued their advance along the ridge: "Further north battalions of the same London and Naval Divisions (58th and 63rd) that had taken part in the attack on 26th October again

FIFTY-EIGHTH DIVISION 157

made progress wherever it was possible to find a way across the swamps. The almost impassable nature of the ground in this area, however, made movement practically impossible, and it was only on the main ridge that much could be effected."

The fine reputation of the Division was enhanced, not only by the fighting qualities displayed in these and other actions, but by the soldierly spirit with which they endured the horrors of the salient throughout an unusually long spell of service there.

When the German offensive opened on 21st March, 1918, the 58th Division was in the III. Corps, Fifth Army; the other divisions of that Corps on the 21st being the 14th on the left and the 18th in the centre. The 58th on the right was the flank unit of the British Armies. The Oise above La Fère, opposite the ground held by the left brigade of the 58th, flows from north to south and thereafter from east to west. One brigade, the 173rd, was on the west bank above the bend while the others held a line from the south bank to Barisis, four miles south of the river. The two latter brigades were not seriously involved on the 21st. Sir Arthur Conan Doyle gives a detailed account of the battle on the III. Corps front. At p. 111, vol. v. he states that the 173rd Brigade, " which filled the space between Travecy on the left, and the Oise upon the right, had the 2/1st Londons in the forward zone, the 2/4th Londons in the battle zone opposite La Fère and the 2/3rd Londons in the rear zone upon the Crozat Canal. The single battalion in front was attacked by the impossible odds of three German divisions but held out for a long time with great constancy." The battalion was overwhelmed but fought to the end. The enemy stormed forward to the battle zone but were vigorously opposed by the 4th Battalion aided by some sappers and pioneers. This force held up the attack for a time but were pressed back. "By 5 a.m. on the 22nd all troops were across, and the bridges destroyed. The 2/4th Londons succeeded in removing all their stores and munitions, and their remarkable achievement in holding the high ground of La Fère against ten times their numbers for as many hours, during which they inflicted very heavy losses upon their assailants, and repulsed six separate attacks, was among the outstanding military feats of that difficult day."

The 18th Division made a wonderfully fine and successful stand, but a break-through occurred on the front of the 14th Division.

Sir Douglas Haig in his despatch of 20th July, 1918, paragraph 10, gives the dispositions of the various Corps on the Fifth Army front and states that "Over ten miles of this front between Amigny Rouy and Alaincourt were protected by the marshes of the Oise river and canal, and were therefore held more lightly than the remainder of the line; but on the whole front of this Army the number of divisions in line only allowed of an average of one division to some 6750 yards of front."

On the III. Corps front the extent of ground held was about 30,000 yards by two divisions and a brigade of a third. Their line was certainly opposite the marsh area but, as pointed out in paragraph 15 of the despatch, "Assisted by the long spell of dry

FIFTY-EIGHTH DIVISION 159

weather hostile infantry had crossed the river and canal north of La Fère, and, south of St. Quentin, had penetrated into the battle zone between Essigny and Benay."

Paragraph 14 shows that during the morning of the 21st, " the enemy had penetrated our front line opposite La Fère." This was in the area of the 58th, see map opposite p. 186 of Messrs. Dent's edition.

Paragraph 16 shows that Fargnier and Quessy were lost during the afternoon and evening of the 21st.

Paragraph 17 states that on the evening of the 21st the Fifth Army Commander decided to "withdraw the divisions of that Corps (the III.) behind the Crozat Canal. . . . These different withdrawals were carried out successfully during the night. . . . Instances of great bravery occurred in the destruction of the bridges."

Paragraph 18: "On the morning of the 22nd March the ground was again enveloped in thick mist, under cover of which the enemy renewed his attacks in great strength all along the line. Fighting was again very heavy, and short-range fire from guns, rifles and machine-guns caused enormous losses to the enemy's troops. The weight of his attack, however, combined with the impossibility of observing beforehand and engaging with artillery the massing of his troops, enabled him to press forward."

Paragraph 19: "In the south the enemy advanced during the morning as far as the line of the canal at Jussy" (area of 18th Division), "and a fierce struggle commenced for the passage of the canal, his troops bringing up trench mortars and machine guns, and endeavouring to cross on rafts under cover of their fire. At 1 p.m. he succeeded in effecting a crossing at Quessy, and made progress during the afternoon in the direction of Vouel. His further advance in this sector, however, was delayed by the gallant resistance of troops of the 58th Division, under command of Major-General A. B. E. Cator, at Tergnier, and it was not until evening, after many costly attempts and much sanguinary fighting, that the enemy gained possession of this village."

On 23rd March the 173rd Brigade had again very heavy fighting about Noureuil. The despatch, paragraph 25, refers to " the most resolute resistance offered to the enemy's advance " by the III. Corps and "many gallant actions performed." The fighting 21st to 23rd March is now the "Battle of St. Quentin."

On the 24th the III. Corps, and certain French troops which had come to its aid, were pushed back to the south and west of Chauny by the huge forces of the enemy (see paragraph 32). That night the remnants of the 173rd brigade were ordered to rejoin the remainder of the Division on the south side of the Oise.

While the British were being pushed back on the north bank, the 174th and 175th Brigades kept extending to their left along the south bank and held the river line, until their frontage was about twelve miles. This task was of absolutely vital importance. Several hostile attempts to cross were defeated.

FIFTY-EIGHTH DIVISION

Mr. Sparrow in his *Fifth Army* does not give details regarding the work of the 58th, but on p. 85 he speaks of their resistance at Tergnier on the 22nd, and in a note there occurs this sentence: "What could have been more valuable to the Allied cause than was this prolonged resistance at a most critical time and place?" On p. 283 there is another note which mentions that the right of the Division was not attacked, "their left had fought magnificently."

The Division was taken north early in April, and was immediately to the south of Villers Bretonneux when that village was captured by the enemy on 24th April. They were heavily engaged on that and the two succeeding days during which the village and certain other positions were recaptured. The Division again had serious losses.

In the telegraphic despatch of 13th September, 1918, as to the work of various divisions, Sir Douglas Haig said: "The 58th Division, which held the right of the British line on March 21st, attacked on August 8th, north of the Somme, and captured Sailly Laurette. In five days of severe fighting the Division captured many prisoners and guns, and performed very gallant service on the left flank of our advance south of the Somme. On the 24th August it again attacked in the sector north of the Somme, and once more did gallant work, overcoming strong hostile resistance at Maricourt and Marrières Wood."

The despatch of 21st December, 1918, shows, paragraph 16, that the 58th was in the III. Corps, Fourth Army, when it was employed in the attack on 8th August. That date and succeeding days are

162 THE TERRITORIAL DIVISIONS

dealt with in paragraphs 15 to 18 of the written despatch. In paragraph 15 Sir Douglas Haig remarked that: "A strong local attack launched by the enemy on the 6th August, south of Morlancourt, led to severe fighting, and undoubtedly rendered the task of the III. Corps more difficult."

On the 8th the 58th took Sailly Laurette, but were held up at Chipilly Spur. With some assistance this was cleared on the 9th. On the 10th a further advance was made by the III. Corps. The fighting 8th–11th August is now designated "The Battle of Amiens."

Paragraph 21 deals with the attack by the III. Corps on 22nd August, the 47th, 12th and 18th of that Corps and the 3rd Australian and 38th Divisions being employed in the first line of attacking troops. The 58th reinforced the 47th in the afternoon. Albert was taken and the left of the Fourth Army brought forward.

Paragraph 22 describes the fighting on 23rd and 24th August when further progress was made. "Divisions which in the worst days of the March retreat had proved themselves superior to every hardship, difficulty and danger, once more rose to the occasion with the most magnificent spirit; over the same ground that had witnessed their stubborn greatness in defence they moved forward to the attack with a persistent vigour and relentless determination which neither the extreme difficulty of the ground, nor the obstinate resistance of the enemy, could diminish or withstand."

The fighting 21st–23rd August is now "The Battle of Albert, 1918."

FIFTY-EIGHTH DIVISION 163

On the 24th the 58th had a stiff fight but they and the 47th secured their objectives.

Paragraph 23 said: "During the next five days our troops followed up their advantage hotly, and in spite of increasing resistance from the German rearguards, realised a further deep advance. The enemy clung to his positions in the latter stages of this period with much tenacity. His infantry delivered many counter-attacks, and the progress of our troops was only won by hard and determined fighting." On 28th August, "the 12th Division and 58th Division (Major-General F. W. Ramsay) captured Hardecourt and the spur south of it, overcoming strong resistance."

On the 25th the 58th were heavily engaged at Billon Wood which was held strongly. On the 28th they took Marrières Wood.

Paragraph 24 deals with the fighting for Mont St. Quentin and the capture of Peronne, in support of which operations the 58th, 47th and other divisions attacked on 31st August, and "by successful fighting on this and the following day, captured Bouchavesnes, Rancourt and Frégicourt, with several hundred prisoners." This is now the "Second Battle of Bapaume."

Paragraph 30 described the Battle of Havrincourt and Epéhy, 12th–18th September, and as to 18th September, the "Battle of Epéhy," said, "On the extreme right, and in the left centre about Epéhy the enemy's resistance was very determined and in these sectors troops of the 6th, 12th, 18th and 58th Divisions had severe fighting. Before nightfall, however, the last centres of resistance in

164 THE TERRITORIAL DIVISIONS

Epéhy were reduced, and both in this area and on our right about Gricourt local actions during the succeeding days secured for us the remainder of the positions required for an attack on the main Hindenburg defences."

On the 18th September the 58th took Peizières and made further progress during the next 48 hours.

On 24th September the Division, now weakened by the heavy tasks it had carried through during eight weeks' fighting, left the III. Corps and moved north to join the First Army. It had no more hard fighting. In October, headquarters of that Corps were transferred to the Fifth Army in Flanders where times were less strenuous.

Major-General Montgomery's *Story of the Fourth Army* (Hodder and Stoughton) contains many flattering references to the work of the Division in August and September, 1918.

59TH (NORTH MIDLAND) DIVISION

SECOND LINE

THIS Division was employed in Ireland at the time of the Dublin rebellion of April 1916, and, but for that outbreak, might have gone abroad earlier than it did. It sailed in February 1917, was taken to the district east of Amiens and assisted to press the enemy when he retreated in March of that year. When the retreat was over they occupied the line near Havrincourt Wood; at that time they formed part of the III. Corps, Fourth Army. On 13th April, the 59th and other troops made an advance when ground near Gricourt was taken and consolidated.

In the autumn of 1917 the Division was in the Ypres salient, and was employed as part of the V. Corps about the Wieltje—Gravenstafel road, east of St. Julien, in the attack of 26th September, now called the " Battle of Polygon Wood," a stage in the Third Battle of Ypres, when, at the cost of heavy losses various strong points were captured and the line advanced. A quotation as to this from the despatch of 25th December, 1917, paragraph 52, has already been given under the 58th Division, see also map opposite p. 123 of Messrs. Dent's edition of *Sir Douglas Haig's Despatches*.

The map opposite p. 163 of the same edition shows that the 59th was at Cantaing, south-west of Cambrai, when the enemy made their great counter-attack on 30th November, 1917, but it was not so severely pressed at that point as on the immediate left of the Division.

The Division was heavily involved in the great German offensive—the " Battle of St. Quentin "— which commenced on 21st March, 1918, and had very severe losses. The map opposite p. 186 of the edition above referred to shows that the Division was occupying the line about Bullecourt in the area of the Third Army on the 21st and a break-through took place between Bullecourt and Lagnicourt, the latter place being in the area of the 6th Division on the immediate right of the 59th. This part of the line was evidently one of those selected by the enemy for a special effort, five divisions attacking the 59th and a portion of the 34th on its left. Sir Arthur Conan Doyle gives an excellent account of this part of the great battle; he states that the 178th and 176th brigades were in the front line. These were destroyed but the 177th in support beat off three very heavy attacks and held out till assistance came from a division in reserve, the 40th. The 177th Brigade remained with the 40th Division and saw further intense fighting during the next few days—the " First Battle of Bapaume." Sir Arthur, vol. v., p. 77, puts the losses of the Division in the March battle at 5765.

The Division was taken to Flanders and was involved in the " Battles of the Lys," in April. Sir Arthur Conan Doyle, in the volume above referred to, draws attention to the excellent work of the 178th (Sherwood Forester) Brigade, when attached to other divisions about 12th to 14th April, but as a whole the Division was still suffering from the grievous losses sustained three weeks before; that period being obviously insufficient to assimilate the new drafts which formed such a large proportion of the total strength.

In consequence of the very heavy casualties it had suffered in the March battle and on the Lys the Division was reduced to a cadre basis (see note to despatch of 21st December, 1918, paragraph 1, Dent's edition), but it recuperated in time to take part in the final British offensive.

In the despatch of 21st December, 1918, paragraph 45, it is stated that on 17th October, 1918, the 57th and 59th Divisions of the XI. Corps were on the outskirts of Lille. On the 18th Lille " was clear of the enemy," and our line was carried far to the east. " Thereafter our troops pressed forward steadily."

60TH (2ND LONDON) DIVISION

SECOND LINE

THE 60th Division went to France in June 1916. Their first experience at the front was in the Arras district. They were there initiated in trench warfare by the 51st Division, before the latter moved south to take part in the great conflict on the Somme.

After about six months in the line on the Western Front the 60th were, in January 1917, sent to Salonika. There they saw some hard fighting in May. In June they joined the Egyptian Expeditionary Force for service in Palestine. In that country, as will be seen from the extracts given below, they earned great distinction.

Sir E. Allenby's despatch of 16th December, 1917, recounting the operations which culminated in the surrender of Jerusalem, shows that the Division bore a most important and honourable share of the heavy task that fell to his troops.

The attack was to commence with the capture of Beersheba, situated on the eastern or left flank of the Turkish position, on 31st October, 1917. The despatch says, paragraph 8: "As a preliminary to the main attack, in order to enable field guns to be brought within effective range for wire-cutting, the enemy's advanced works at 1070 were to be taken. This was successfully accomplished at

8.45 a.m., after a short preliminary bombardment by London troops, with small loss, 90 prisoners being taken. . . . The final assault was ordered for 12.15 p.m.; it was successful all along the front attacked."

Beersheba was taken at 7 p.m. on the 31st, the Australian Light Horse and Yeomanry doing very well. The despatch states: "The Turks at Beersheba were undoubtedly taken completely by surprise, a surprise from which the dash of London troops and Yeomanry, finely supported by their artillery, never gave them time to recover. The charge by the Australian Light Horse completed their defeat." About 2000 prisoners and 13 guns were taken and 500 Turkish corpses buried. The enemy's left flank was laid bare.

Paragraph 11: On 6th November the Kauwukah system of trenches was attacked. Yeomanry first stormed the works on the left; "soon after noon the London and Irish troops commenced their attack. It was completely successful in capturing all its objectives and the whole of the Rushdi system in addition. . . . This attack was a fine performance, the troops advancing eight or nine miles during the day and capturing a series of very strong works covering a front of about seven miles, the greater part of which had been held and strengthened by the enemy for over six months. Some 600 prisoners and some guns and machine guns were captured. Our casualties were comparatively slight."

Paragraph 12: On the 7th November "the London troops, after a severe engagement at Tel el

SIXTIETH DIVISION

Sheria, which they captured by a bayonet charge, at 4 a.m. on the 7th, subsequently repulsing several counter-attacks, pushed forward their line about a mile to the north." The operations of 27th October to 7th November are now the "Third Battle of Gaza."

For some weeks the strain on the troops was very great, much heavy marching on a short supply of water having to be undertaken in addition to constant fighting, which during the last half of November became much more intense. Aided by reinforcements and by the mountainous nature of the country the enemy put up a great effort to bring the advance to a standstill, but in this he failed.

The assault on the positions defending Jerusalem was fixed for 8th December, the 60th being again employed. The despatch draws attention to "the mere physical difficulties of the advance across steep and rocky hillsides and deep valleys," artillery support being difficult, indeed sometimes impossible, while "the opposition encountered was considerable." The weather was most unfavourable, rain falling heavily on the 7th and three following days.

The first objectives were carried soon after dawn and the troops pressed on. "By about noon London troops had already advanced over two miles, and were swinging north-east to gain the Nablus—Jerusalem road," "throwing back their right to form a defensive flank, facing east towards Jerusalem, from the western outskirts of which considerable rifle and artillery fire was being experienced. . . .

By nightfall . . . all the enemy's prepared defences west and north-west of Jerusalem had been captured. . . . The London troops and Yeomanry had displayed great endurance in difficult conditions. The London troops, especially, after a night march in heavy rain to reach their positions of deployment, had made an advance of three to four miles in difficult hills in the face of stubborn opposition."

On the 9th the advance was resumed, the London troops and Yeomanry driving back rearguards. At noon the city was surrendered. The Army had taken over 12,000 prisoners and 100 guns between 31st October and 9th December. (See also under 52nd, 53rd and 54th Divisions.)

Sir E. Allenby's despatch of 18th September, 1918, shows that after the surrender of Jerusalem, he desired to drive back the enemy further from its precincts.

Paragraph 5: While the XX. Corps, which included the 53rd and 60th Divisions, was making preparations to do this the Turks attacked during the night of 26th–27th December. " By 1.30 a.m. the 60th Division was engaged on its whole front.

" Between 1.30 a.m. and 8 a.m. on the 27th the outposts of the 60th Division on the ridge north of Beit Hanninah repelled four determined attacks, but the heaviest fighting took place to the east of the Jerusalem—Nablus road. Repeated attacks were made against Tel el Ful; a conspicuous hill from which Jerusalem and the intervening ground can be overlooked. The attacks were made by picked bodies of troops and were pressed with great

SIXTIETH DIVISION

determination. At only one point did the enemy succeed in reaching the main line of defence. He was driven out at once by the local reserves. In all these attacks he lost heavily."

After a lull the enemy attacked the front of the 60th Division at 12.55 p.m. "in unexpected strength," but again "local counter-attacks were successful in restoring the line—this proved to be the final effort."

On the 28th December, General Allenby ordered an advance. The battle was of a very obstinate character and lasted into the evening of the 29th. On the 28th the 60th captured several strong positions by 1 p.m., further positions by 5.30 p.m. and continued their advance till 9.15 p.m. On the 29th they resumed their forward movement, meeting heavy rifle and machine-gun fire near Bireh. About 4.15 p.m., "the left of the attack stormed the Tahuneh ridge." "Simultaneously with this attack the right of the 60th Division had stormed Shab Saleh in face of heavy machine-gun fire; subsequently capturing the ridge east of Bireh. At 9 p.m. the advance was continued."

"The Turkish attempt to recapture Jerusalem had thus ended in crushing defeat. He had employed fresh troops who had not participated in the recent retreat from Beersheba and Gaza and had escaped its demoralising effects. The determination and gallantry with which his attack was carried out only served to increase his losses."

Another quotation as to this battle has been given under the 53rd Division, which was also in the XX. Corps. The operations 17th–24th November, 1917, are now the "Battle of Nebi Samwil," and those 26th to 30th December, the "Defence of Jerusalem."

Paragraphs 6 and 7 of the despatch deal with the advance to and capture of Jericho and give a detailed description of the immense difficulties which the troops had to surmount.

"The 60th Division had taken over the line east of Jerusalem some time previously. Opposed to it were some 5000 rifles, while to the north another 2000 rifles were in a position from which to act against the left flank of the 60th Division as it advanced.

"The chief obstacle to the advance lay in the difficulty of the ground rather than any opposition the enemy might offer."

Between the line of the 60th and their objectives lay a succession of ridges some of which were precipitous.

The advance on Jericho began on 19th February, 1918. On that day the Division captured several strong positions " in face of considerable opposition."

That night the enemy attacked and was repulsed " after a sharp struggle."

On the 20th further positions were taken, " the enemy resisting with stubbornness. . . . The right brigade met with great opposition. Moreover, the ground over which the attack had to take place proved the most rugged and difficult yet met with in this country. . . . The left brigade advanced four miles over difficult country, the enemy fighting a rearguard action from ridge to ridge."

By the evening of the 20th " the 60th Division had reached a line four miles west of the cliffs overlooking Jericho."

SIXTIETH DIVISION 175

On the 21st the advance was resumed, the Division reaching a line which overlooked Jericho. At 8.20 a.m. mounted troops rode into the town.

Paragraph 8 describes a further advance, 8th to 12th March, in which the XX. Corps " had to drive the enemy from ridge to ridge." On the 9th the right brigade of the 60th Division, which had crossed the Wadi el Auja, north of Jericho, in the dark, and " had subsequently met with determined resistance," seized a position astride the Beisan—Jericho road. Other troops on their left also made good progress and by the 11th " a line had been captured with great natural facilities for defence."

Paragraph 11 and 12 deal with a raid on Amman. The troops employed were the 60th Division, the Australian and New Zealand Mounted Division, the Imperial Camel Brigade, etc., the whole under the General Officer Commanding 60th Division. Heavy rains made the crossing of the Jordan a task of almost insuperable difficulty and also made progress very slow when the eastern bank was reached. On 24th March the 60th Division drove the enemy from a position which blocked the road to Es Salt, captured three guns and pursued him for four miles. On the 25th they occupied Es Salt. The mounted troops effected the destruction of portions of the railway. There was heavy fighting on the 29th and 30th March, the Turks having been reinforced; thereafter the Commander-in-Chief ordered a withdrawal and this was carried out by the evening of 2nd April. Troops were left on the east side of the Jordan to form a bridgehead. Over 900 prisoners were taken in this raid.

176 THE TERRITORIAL DIVISIONS

On 30th April operations east of the Jordan were again undertaken. "The 60th Division captured the advanced works of the Shunet Nimrin position but were unable to make further progress in face of the stubborn resistance offered by the enemy." On 2nd May there was another attack but the Turks were found to be in great strength. "The 60th Division was unable to make any substantial progress, in spite of determined efforts." About 1000 prisoners were taken in this operation. On 4th May the force was withdrawn.

Paragraph 15 of the despatch refers to the reorganisation of the Palestine Army consequent on the departure of the 52nd and 74th Divisions for France, and it states that 24 British battalions were also withdrawn from the remaining divisions and sent to France. The 60th contributed its share of these, while the remainder of the Division continued to set a very high standard of efficient work in the field to the troops brought to Palestine from Mesopotamia and India, to take the place of those who had left for the western front. The 2/20th joined the famous 62nd Division in August 1918.

In the despatch of 31st October, 1918, as to the final overthrow of the Turks in Palestine, paragraph 9 shows that the break-through by the infantry was entrusted to Sir E. Bulfin's XXI. Corps, to which the 60th Division was attached, it having been moved from the right to the left of the line. At 4.30 a.m. on 19th September, the XXI. Corps attacked and, within 36 hours, "the greater part of the VIII. Turkish Army had been overwhelmed."

The 60th Division attacked in the coastal sector,

SIXTIETH DIVISION

then moved inland to leave " the coast route clear for the Desert Mounted Corps."

After the 20th the infantry had heavy marching but no severe fighting. The operations 19th–25th September are now " The Battles of Megiddo."

The armistice with Turkey came into force on 31st October, but fighting had ceased on the 26th. The 60th Division had certainly done a great deal to bring about the satisfactory conclusion of the War with Turkey.

Battalions of the Division were selected for the Armies of Occupation as follows: for Western Front, the 2/14th, 2/15th, 2/16th, 2/17th and 2/23rd London Regiment; for Egypt, 2/13th, 2/19th and 2/22nd London Regiment.

61ST (SOUTH MIDLAND) DIVISION

Second Line

The Division went to France in May 1916. On 19th-20th July they and an Australian division made an attack in the Neuve Chapelle district. Ground was gained but could not be held as the guns on the Aubers Ridge had command of it.

The despatch from Sir Douglas Haig, dated 31st May, 1917, paragraph 13, Messrs. Dent's edition, shows that the 61st was one of the divisions employed in pursuing and pressing the enemy when he retreated from the neighbourhood of the Somme battlefield in March 1917. On 17th March the 61st and 2nd Australian Divisions captured Chaulnes and Bapaume.

The Division was for a time in the Third Battle of Ypres and, as part of the XIX. Corps, attacked on 22nd and 27th August and 5th September, 1917.

The Cambrai despatch of 20th February, 1918, paragraph 9 (Dent's edition) and map opposite p. 163, shows that the 61st was in reserve on 30th November, 1917, when the enemy made his great counter-attack. On the night of the 1st December they took over from the 12th in the neighbourhood of La Vacquerie and for some days thereafter had to fight hard to stem the German flood; in this they were successful.

The Division saw a great deal of heavy fighting in 1918 and was frequently mentioned in despatches. It formed part of the XVIII. Corps, Fifth Army, in March of that year and was engaged throughout the whole of the British retreat. At the end of ten days' continuous fighting the strength of the Division was down to about 2000. They came out of the battle with a splendid reputation, which was to be enhanced later, on the Lys.

In the telegraphic despatch of 26th March, 1918, Sir Douglas Haig said: "In the past six days of constant fighting our troops on all parts of the battle-front have shown the utmost courage," and among divisions which had exhibited "exceptional gallantry" he mentioned the 61st.

In the written despatch of 20th July, 1918, paragraph 15, which deals with the 21st March, it is stated: "Assisted by the long spell of dry weather hostile infantry had crossed the river and canal north of La Fère, and, south of St. Quentin, had penetrated into the battle-zone between Essigny and Benay. At Maissemy, also, our battle positions were entered at about noon, but the vigorous resistance of the 61st and 24th Divisions, assisted by troops of the 1st Cavalry Division, prevented the enemy from developing his success."

The Division held its battle position intact against the assaults of three German divisions, and only retired in the afternoon of the 22nd when ordered to do so in consequence of the enemy's progress at other parts of the line.

In his *History of the British Campaign in France and Flanders*, vol. v., Sir Arthur Conan Doyle gives a full account of the very arduous work of the XVIII. Corps in the March retreat, and frequently refers to the conduct of the 61st Division in terms of very high praise. He gives a detailed description of the most heroic resistance of the battalions in the front line on the morning of 21st March and, as an example of what was done, he tells the story of the 2/4th Oxfordshire and Buckinghamshire Light Infantry which, under Colonel Wetherall, held out in the Enghien Redoubt until it was finally submerged by the ever increasing waves from the three German divisions which attacked the front of the 61st. This took place about 4.30 p.m.

Mr. Sparrow in his *The Fifth Army in March 1918*, also gives many particulars of the splendid defence put up by the forward battalions of the 61st, on the 21st, as well as of the endless encounters they had during the retreat. On p. 239 he mentions that parts of the Division were first attacked at 5 a.m. on the 21st, and were only two miles back at 3 a.m. on the 23rd, although for 48 hours the 61st was attacked by three German divisions. On p. 102 he refers to it as " this brave Division " and says that a Special Order of the day, dated 18th April, stated that between 21st March and that date the 61st had been opposed by 14 German divisions.

At p. 287 Mr. Sparrow remarks that the 61st had been continuously in the line since 27th August, 1917, except when moving from one part to another, and " then fought for twelve continuous days."

Paragraph 24 of the despatch states that on the

morning of the 23rd the Commander of the Fifth Army ordered " a gradual withdrawal to the line of the Somme."

Paragraph 26: A gap occurred in our line near Ham and bodies of Germans succeeded in crossing the river. " In the afternoon these forces increased in strength, gradually pressing back our troops, until a spirited counter-attack by troops of the 20th and 61st Divisions about Verlaines restored the situation in this locality."

The fighting between 21st–23rd March is now designated the " Battle of St. Quentin."

Paragraph 31, " The Fight for the Somme Crossings ": On the 24th various bodies of the enemy had been able to effect crossings at different points. " During the remainder of the day the enemy repeated his attacks at these and other points, and also exercised strong pressure in a westerly and southwesterly direction from Ham. Our troops offered a vigorous resistance and opposite Ham a successful counter-attack by the 1/5th (Pioneer) Battalion, Duke of Cornwall's Light Infantry, 61st Division, materially delayed his advance."

Paragraph 44: On 28th March the British were almost back to the Amiens defences and the enemy were seriously pressing the French on our right. "A gallant attempt by troops of the 61st Division to regain Warfusée-Abancourt and lighten the pressure from the north proved unsuccessful. . . . At nightfall we held approximately the Amiens defence line on the whole front south of the Somme."

Fortunately that same day the enemy had been defeated north of the Somme (see 56th, 42nd and

SIXTY-FIRST DIVISION 183

62nd Divisions), and in a few days his offensive on the front south of Arras ceased.

In his account of the 28th, Mr. Sparrow deals with the work of "the intrepid 61st," and remarks "one and all behaved with the greatest gallantry."

In Colonel à Court Repington's Memoirs, *The First World War*, Constable, vol. ii., p. 269, there is detailed a conversation, on 7th April, 1918, with General Gough, the Commander of the Fifth Army. After some particulars of the great struggle there occurs the sentence, "He brought with him some of Maxse's notes, which mentioned particularly the fine conduct of the 61st Division, under Colin Mackenzie." Lieut.-General Maxse commanded the XVIII. Corps.

The despatch of 20th July, 1918, deals also with the Lys battle which began on 9th April, 1918 (see 55th, 49th, 50th and 51st Divisions). Paragraph 58 shows that several divisions were brought straight from the Somme fighting to the Lys area. Among these was the 61st. Dealing with the 12th April, the despatch states: "On the left of the 51st the 61st Division was coming into action about the Clarence river. Both the 3rd and 61st Divisions had been engaged in many days of continuous fighting south of Arras; but with the arrival of these troops, battle-weary though they were, the enemy's progress in this sector was definitely checked."

The fighting 12th–15th April is now the "Battle of Hazebrouck."

Paragraph 65 deals with the great effort made by the enemy on 18th April on the southern front of his salient. "At certain points there was severe and continuous fighting. . . . Elsewhere the enemy failed to obtain even an initial success, being repulsed, with exceedingly heavy loss, at all points, by the 4th and 61st Divisions." And, referring to a few days later: "Further west the 4th Division, in co-operation with the 61st Division, carried out a series of successful local operations, north of the La Bassée canal, resulting in the capture of some hundreds of prisoners, and a considerable improvement of our positions between the Lawe and Clarence rivers." The action on 18th April is now the " Battle of Béthune."

The Division joined the XVII. Corps early in October 1918, and with it took part in the " Advance to Victory."

The despatch of 21st December, 1918, as to the final British offensive, paragraph 47, Battle of the Selle River, 17th–25th October, shows that the 61st Division, as part of the XVII. Corps of the Third Army, attacked on 24th October. " About many of the woods and villages which lay in the way of our attack there was severe fighting, particularly in the large wood known as the Bois L'Évêque, and at Pommereuil, Bousies Forest and Vendegies-sur-Écaillon. This latter village held out till the afternoon of the 24th October when it was taken by an enveloping attack by troops of the 19th Division and 61st Division."

Paragraph 49, " The Battle of the Sambre," 1st–11th November: As a preliminary to the main attack it is stated that on 1st November " the XVII. Corps of the Third Army and the XXII. and Canadian Corps of the First Army attacked on a front of about six miles south of Valenciennes and in the course of two days of heavy fighting inflicted a severe defeat on the enemy. During these two days the 61st, Major-General F. J. Duncan, 49th and 4th Divisions crossed the Rhonelle river, capturing Maresches and Preseau after a stubborn struggle, and established themselves on the high ground two miles to the east of it. On their left the 4th Canadian Division captured Valenciennes and made progress beyond the town."

The fighting on 1st–2nd November is now designated the " Battle of Valenciennes."

On the 3rd November the enemy withdrew, and the British line was advanced.

The XVII. Corps was again employed on the left of the Third Army in the Battle of the Sambre on the 4th November when " the enemy's resistance was definitely broken."

Battalions from the Division were selected for the Armies of Occupation, as follows: Western Front, 2/6th and 2/7th Royal Warwickshire Regiment 2/5th Gloucestershire Regiment and 1/5th Duke of Cornwall's Light Infantry (Pioneers). For Egypt, 2/8th Worcestershire Regiment, 2/4th Oxfordshire and Buckinghamshire Light Infantry and 2/4th Royal Berkshire Regiment.

62ND (WEST RIDING) DIVISION
SECOND LINE

THE 62nd Division, under the command of Major-General W. P. Braithwaite, who had gained distinction as chief of Sir Ian Hamilton's staff in Gallipoli, left England for France on 11th January, 1917, and, on arrival, was taken to the Albert—Arras area. On 13th February they entered the line about Serre, thereafter until the end of March they were one of the divisions employed in pressing the enemy, and in causing him to hasten his withdrawal from the old Somme front. The pursuit came to a standstill near Bullecourt on the Hindenburg line. The capture of that place was to involve much hard fighting. The Division at this time was in the V. Corps, Fifth Army.

Sir Douglas Haig's despatch of 25th December, 1917, as to the campaigns of that year, paragraph 16 (Dent's edition), describes the fighting on 11th April in the Battle of Arras. " In combination with this attack on the Third Army front, the Fifth Army launched an attack at 4.30 a.m. on the 11th April against the Hindenburg Line in the neighbourhood of Bullecourt (4th Australian Division and 62nd Division, Major-Generals W. Holmes and W. P. Braithwaite). The Australian and West Riding battalions engaged showed great gallantry in executing a very difficult attack across a wide extent of open country. Considerable progress was made and parties of Australian troops, preceded by tanks, penetrated the German positions as far as Riencourt-lez-Cagnicourt." As the Third Army was held up on this day the Fifth Army had to withdraw. Progress was made on the 12th.

Paragraph 27: " To secure the footing gained by the Australians in the Hindenburg Line on 3rd May it was advisable that Bullecourt should be captured without loss of time. . . . On the morning of the 7th May English troops (7th Division) gained a footing in the south-east corner of Bullecourt. Thereafter gradual progress was made in the face of the most obstinate resistance and on the 17th May London and West Riding Territorials (58th and 62nd Divisions) completed the capture of the village." The operations 3rd to 17th May are now the " Battle of Bullecourt."

Throughout the summer of 1917 the 62nd remained in the district south of Arras, but had no heavy fighting until the " Battle of Cambrai, 1917."

Sir Douglas Haig's despatch of 20th February, 1918, as to the " Battle of Cambrai, 1917," 20th November to 3rd December, paragraph 3, dealing with the attack on 20th November, said: " The 62nd (West Riding) Division, T., stormed Havrincourt where also parties of the enemy held out for a time. . . . West of Flesquières the 62nd Division operating northwards from Havrincourt made important progress. Having carried the Hindenburg reserve line north of that village it rapidly continued its attack and captured Graincourt, where two anti-tank guns were destroyed

SIXTY-SECOND DIVISION 189

by the tanks accompanying our infantry. Before nightfall infantry and cavalry had entered Anneux although the enemy's resistance in this village does not appear to have been finally overcome until the following morning. This attack of the 62nd (West Riding) Division constitutes a brilliant achievement in which the troops concerned completed an advance of four and a half miles from their original front, overrunning two German systems of defence and gaining possession of three villages."

Paragraph 4, 21st November, stated: "Following upon the capture of Flesquières the 51st and 62nd Divisions, in co-operation with a number of tanks and squadrons of the 1st Cavalry Division, attacked at 10.30 a.m. in the direction of Fontaine-Notre-Dame and Bourlon." After drawing attention to the strain on the troops engaged in these operations Sir Douglas Haig said, paragraph 7: "It was decided to make another effort on 27th November to capture Fontaine-Notre-Dame and Bourlon village," etc. "In this attack in which tanks co-operated, British Guards temporarily regained possession of Fontaine, taking some hundreds of prisoners, and troops of the 62nd Division once more entered Bourlon village. Later in the morning, however, heavy counter-attacks developed in both localities and our troops were unable to maintain the ground they had gained." The Division was relieved by the 47th on the night of the 28th–29th. It was in reserve on the 30th November when the enemy counter-attacked in great force—see paragraph 9 of despatch, also under 47th, 55th, and 56th Divisions.

190 THE TERRITORIAL DIVISIONS

In the beginning of 1918, the Division was about Arras, on 5th January it took over from the 56th between Gavrelle and Oppy.

Soon after the launching of the German attack from the St. Quentin district, on 21st March, reinforcements were sent to the southern portions of the British front. On 25th March the 62nd Division arrived at Bucquoy and joined the IV. Corps of the Third Army. Along with the 42nd Division they formed a new line through which the worn-out 19th, 25th, 41st and 51st Divisions withdrew. The 62nd, which entered the front line on the 25th, had very heavy fighting on the 26th, 27th and 28th. On the afternoon of the 26th alone five attacks by regiments of the Prussian Guard were repulsed. After a magnificent stand the Division was relieved by the 37th on 31st March and 1st April. The fighting on 24th–25th is now the " First Battle of Bapaume," and that on the 28th the " First Battle of Arras, 1918."

Under the 42nd Division a quotation has already been given from the telegraphic despatch of 23rd April, 1918, in which the part played by the 42nd and 62nd about Bucquoy is referred to.

The written despatch of 20th July, 1918, paragraph 42, mentions that on 27th March the enemy made a series of strong attacks when he gained Ablainzevelle and Ayette. " Elsewhere all his assaults were heavily repulsed by troops of the 62nd Division (Major-General W. P. Braithwaite) and of the 42nd and the Guards Divisions."

Paragraph 45 as to the attack near Arras, 28th March, states: " The 62nd Division with an attached brigade of the 4th Australian Division beat off a succession of heavy attacks about Bucquoy with great loss to the enemy."

The despatch of 21st December, 1918, paragraph 11, shows that in July the XXII. Corps, Lieut.-General Sir A. Godley, consisting of the 15th, 34th, 51st and 62nd Divisions, was sent to the south to assist the French in their counter-attacks against the salient which the Germans had created between the Aisne and the Marne. The 51st and 62nd went to the east side of the salient and had heavy fighting for a period of ten days—a quotation as to this, now the " Battle of Tardenois," is given under the 51st. Both these divisions were complimented by General Berthelot commanding the French Fifth Army. The 8th West Yorkshire Regiment (Leeds Rifles) of the 62nd were awarded the coveted *Croix de Guerre* with palms, for a brilliant assault on Mont de Bligny on 28th July.

In the supplementary telegraphic despatch of 13th September, 1918, as to the work of certain divisions, Sir Douglas Haig said: " The 62nd Division assisted to check the enemy's advance in March at Achiet-le-Grand and Bucquoy and since that date took part with credit in the French offensive south-west of Reims. On August 25th it attacked and captured Mory. The Division was involved in heavy fighting about this village and around Vaulx-Vraucourt and Vaulx Wood and beat off several determined counter-attacks with great loss to the enemy." The capture of Mory is again referred to in the despatch of 21st December, 1918, paragraph 23. Between the 25th August and 2nd September the Division had some very stern fighting and suffered heavy losses before its opponents were overcome. The fighting 31st August–3rd September is now the " Second Battle of Bapaume."

Paragraph 30 of the despatch, " The Battle of Havrincourt and Epéhy 12th–18th September," stated: " On the 12th September the IV. and VI. Corps of the Third Army attacked on a front of about five miles in the Havrincourt sector, employing troops of the New Zealand, 37th, 62nd and 2nd Divisions. The villages of Trescault and Havrincourt were taken by the 37th and 62nd Divisions respectively, and positions were secured which were of considerable importance in view of future operations." This is now designated the " Battle of Havrincourt." It will be remembered that the Division stormed Havrincourt in the battle of 20th November, 1917. It was on familiar ground.

In " The Battle of Cambrai and the Hindenburg Line, 27th September–5th October," the VI. Corps was again employed, the 62nd being in support of the 3rd Division. (See paragraph 35 of the despatch and map opposite p. 280 of Messrs. Dent's edition.) On 27th and 28th September the 62nd captured Marcoing and Masnières and established a bridgehead on the St. Quentin canal. On the 29th they made a further advance. The Official List has altered the designation given in the despatch. This is now the " Battle of the Canal du Nord, 27th September–1st October."

Paragraph 46. " The Battle of the Selle River, 17th–25th October," shows that the 62nd was one of the divisions employed on the 20th. The fighting was severe but all objectives were gained on the high ground east of the river. A quotation as to this action has been given under the 42nd Division. Unofficial accounts agree that both the 42nd and 62nd did particularly well on the 20th October about Solesmes.

Paragraph 50, "The Battle of the Sambre, 1st–11th November," dealing with the 4th November, stated: "Opposite Orsinval the 62nd Division of the VI. Corps attacked at 5.20 a.m., and as soon as that village had been taken the Guards Division of the same corps attacked on the left of them. Both Divisions had hard fighting but made good progress capturing Frasnoy and Preux-au-Sart, and reaching the western outskirts of Commegnies."

Paragraph 51, "The Return to Mons": "The enemy's resistance was definitely broken. On the 9th November the enemy was in general retreat on the whole front of the British Armies. The fortress of Maubeuge was entered by the Guards Division and the 62nd Division (Major-General Sir R. D. Whigham), while the Canadians were approaching Mons," which they entered on the 11th, Armistice Day.

The final despatch of 21st March, 1919 (the anniversary of the great German offensive), paragraph 5, gives the composition of the troops selected to form General Plumer's Second Army, for the march into the British sector in the Rhine provinces; to the 62nd Division was awarded the signal honour of representing the Territorial Force. The Commander-in-Chief may have been influenced by many reasons in making this choice, but unless its marks had been "very good" the 62nd would not have been selected.

The 2/4th West Riding Regiment and 2/4th Yorkshire Light Infantry were chosen for the Army of Occupation, as was also the 1/9th Durham Light Infantry, originally belonging to the 50th, but which served as pioneers to the 62nd in 1918.[1]

[1] Much interesting matter regarding the achievements of the 49th and 62nd Divisions will be found in *The West Riding Territorials in the Great War*, by Major L. Magnus. Kegan Paul and Co. Price 15s.

66TH (EAST LANCASHIRE) DIVISION
SECOND LINE

THE Division landed in France in the last week of February 1917, and was employed for some months with the First and Second Armies about the Bethune—Ypres—Nieuport area.

In the last week of September 1917 the 66th was relieved in the Coast Sector by the 42nd, the senior East Lancashire Division. The 66th then moved into the battle area and joined the Fifth Army, east of Ypres. It came suddenly into prominence in October, when the closing stages of the Third Battle of Ypres were being fought.

In his telegraphic despatch of 9th October, Sir Douglas Haig said: " On the right centre a third-line Territorial Division, comprising Manchester, East Lancashire and Lancashire Fusilier Regiments, advanced one mile northwards along the ridge in the direction of Passchendaele, capturing all its objectives under the most trying and difficult circumstances with great determination and gallantry."

It was not a " third-line " division in the ordinary acceptance of the words, but it did contain a third-line battalion, the 3/5th Lancashire Fusiliers, who were said to have done exceptionally well.

A quotation from paragraph 56 of the written despatch of 25th December, 1917, as to this attack,

196 THE TERRITORIAL DIVISIONS

now designated the "Battle of Poelcappelle," has been given under the 48th Division.

During the German offensive and British retreat of March 1918 the 66th formed part of the XIX. Corps, Fifth Army, the other division of the Corps in the line on 21st March being the 24th.

On the 21st the XIX. Corps was attacked by the enemy in overwhelming force. Both divisions fought splendidly and although their forward posts were surrounded and eventually destroyed, the battle zone of the Corps was held throughout the day. The enemy made progress, however, round the left or north flank of the 66th, and the right or south flank of the 24th Division, which compelled a withdrawal.

In the telegraphic despatch of 26th March, 1918, Sir Douglas Haig said: "In the past six days of constant fighting our troops on all parts of the battle front have shown the utmost courage," and among divisions which had shown "exceptional gallantry" he mentioned the 66th.

Sir Douglas Haig's written despatch of 20th July, 1918, regarding the great German offensive, paragraph 20, the position of affairs on the 22nd March, stated: "At midday, after heavy fighting in the neighbourhood of Roisel, the 66th Division, under the command of Major-General N. Malcolm, D.S.O., still held their positions in this sector, having, for the time being, definitely stopped the enemy's advance. To the south and north, however, the progress of the German infantry continued, . . . Roisel being threatened from the rear. Accordingly our troops about Roisel were withdrawn during the

SIXTY-SIXTH DIVISION 197

afternoon under orders, the enemy making no attempt to interfere." The fighting 21st–23rd March, 1918, is now the "Battle of St. Quentin."

In paragraph 43, regarding the fight for the Rosières line on 27th March, now the "Battle of Rosières," it was said by Sir Douglas Haig that "the situation south of the Somme was serious." "A counter-attack by the 66th Division restored the situation about Framerville."

In paragraph 47 as to the fighting in the Avre and Luce valleys, on 29th and 30th March, Sir Douglas Haig said, "North of the Luce also the enemy made some progress but in the afternoon was held up, and finally driven back into Aubercourt by counter-attacks carried out by troops of the 66th Division and the 3rd Australian Division."

In his "Fifth Army in March, 1918," Mr. Sparrow constantly refers to the splendid conduct of the 66th. At p. 101 he mentions that they fought continuously from the 21st to the 31st and that their losses were nearly 7000 "apart from sick and spent." At p. 134 he says that their strength on the evening of the 30th was 104 officers and 2376 other ranks, excluding transport. "Thus to the last the 66th was in the fire," and speaking of the counter-attack which they made on the 30th he said, "seldom have exhausted men made an equal effort."

Their losses were so severe that the Division was reduced to a cadre basis, see note, paragraph 1, despatch of 21st December, 1918 (Messrs. Dent's edition); but it was filled up in time to take part in the "Advance to Victory."

The South African Brigade, which had gained

198 THE TERRITORIAL DIVISIONS

very great distinction on many occasions, as part of the 9th Division, was incorporated in the reconstituted 66th, and it was also joined by the following battalions from the Mediterranean: the 6th Lancashire Fusiliers 5th Royal Inniskilling Fusiliers, and 6th Royal Dublin Fusiliers, forming the 198th Brigade; the 18th Liverpool Regiment (formerly Lancashire Yeomanry), 9th Manchester Regiment and 5th Connaught Rangers, forming the 199th Brigade, with, as pioneers, the 9th Gloucestershire Regiment. (See *The Story of the Fourth Army*, p. 322.)

The despatch of 21st December, 1918, paragraph 42, " Second Battle of Le Cateau, 8th to 12th October," now officially designated the " Battle of Cambrai, 1918, with pursuit to the Selle," shows that the Division formed part of the troops attacking on 8th October, being then in the XIII. Corps, Fourth Army, when " on the British front infantry and tanks penetrated the enemy's position to a depth of between three and four miles, passing rapidly over the incomplete trench lines."

To the north of the 30th American Division which had " captured Brancourt and Prémont the 66th Division (Major-General H. K. Bethell), attacking beside the 25th Division (Major-General J. R. E. Charles), captured Serain." The advance was continued on the 9th; " by nightfall our troops were within two miles of Le Cateau." A further forward movement was made on the 10th and in *The History of the 25th Division*, p. 329, it is stated that by the evening of the 10th " the 66th Division, which had got well forward on the left, had a few advanced

SIXTY-SIXTH DIVISION 199

patrols in Le Cateau itself." This is correct, but there was to be very heavy fighting before the town was captured. The Selle runs through the town, and the portion on the eastern side of the river was not taken till the 17th.

Paragraph 46, "The forcing of the Selle River crossings, 17th–25th October," now the "Battle of the Selle," mentions the 66th as again employed by the XIII. Corps. "The enemy was holding the difficult wooded country east of Bohain and the line of the Selle north of it, in great strength, his infantry being well supported by artillery. . . . By the evening of the 19th October, after much severe fighting, the enemy had been driven across the Sambre and Oise canal at practically all points south of Catillon, whence our line followed the valley of the Richemont east and north of Le Cateau." That town was taken by the 66th Division.

On the night of the 16th the 9th Gloucestershire, Pioneers to the Division, and the Divisional Engineers threw eight bridges across the Selle, here twenty feet wide and five feet deep, and the South African Brigade crossed to the east bank. Later they forced their way through the wire entanglements and carried their objectives. In the *Story of the Fourth Army*, p. 224, there occurs this sentence: "The position attacked by the 66th Division, and especially by the South African Brigade, requires to be studied on the ground before the difficulties overcome by the initiative and leadership of the regimental officers and non-commissioned officers, and by the gallantry of all ranks, can be fully realised. None but the very best troops could have attempted, let alone have succeeded in, such an enterprise, and the crossing of the Selle at Le Cateau will always remain, like the struggle in Delville Wood in 1916, a lasting testimony to the fighting qualities of the South African soldier." A captured German order contained the sentence: " The English must not cross the Selle on our front."

Sir A. Conan Doyle, vol. vi. pp. 187–190, gives a detailed and excellent account of the attack on 17th October. He says: " It had been a very desperate battle, the laurels of which rest with the South African Brigade, who had carried out so remarkable an assault, and also with the 50th Division which had held on with such a bull-dog grip to its purpose."

The XIII. Corps was engaged in " The Battle of the Sambre," commencing on 4th November, the 66th being in support of the 25th, which captured Landrecies. (See under 48th Division, three battalions of which did great work.) See also paragraph 50 of the despatch and map opposite p. 294 of Messrs. Dent's edition.

On 7th November the 66th relieved the 25th and continued the advance beyond Avesnes, being practically advance-guard to the Fourth Army. At the date of the Armistice the Division held the front from Sivry to a point west of Beaumont.

The work of the 66th Division between 8th October and 11th November is fully described in *The Story of the Fourth Army* already referred to.

APPENDIX

APPENDIX

Showing the Battles, as named in the Official List published in 1921, in which the Territorial Divisions took part.

Since the foregoing notes were put together there has been published "The Official Names of the Battles and other Engagements fought by the Military Forces of the British Empire during the Great War, 1914–1919, and Third Afghan War, 1919, being the Report of the Battles Nomenclature Committee, as approved by the Army Council."

A list of the battles in which a division has been present affords some idea of its services to the Empire, but opportunities varied according to the theatre, and while the work of those troops which went early to the East was of inestimable importance and while very many of their battalions fought in Mesopotamia, Palestine and elsewhere, they had no chance of employment as divisions in the field, hence, through no fault of their own, their honours as divisions are *nil*. In the case of some which operated in France the urgency of affairs, in the early years of the War, was such as to necessitate their employment as reinforcements in single battalions to Regular brigades, and it must not be forgotten that the component parts of some divisions, such as the 55th and 56th, were nearly a year, more in the case of some battalions, in France before they were concentrated as divisions. In their case again a mere list of battle honours in that

204 THE TERRITORIAL DIVISIONS

formation is inadequate as a token of their value. Some of those so placed seem to have made up lost time splendidly.

It would be presumption to say that the following table is complete. There will be many claims which will require very careful scrutiny, and only the Authorities, with all the material of the Historical Section of the War Office at their disposal, will be competent to adjudicate upon them. On the other hand the despatches do mention certain units, and other works of a semi-official character, already published, supplement the reports of the various Commanders; from such sources a fairly complete list can be made up.

In this Appendix, where a division has been mentioned in despatches or works such as the " Story of the Fourth Army," as taking part in a battle, or is shown in the maps appended to these, the Battle is in ordinary type; but where the information is derived from sources not so strictly official, the name of the Battle is printed in italics. In compiling this appendix it has been thought better not to ask information from units as to their own doings.

The geographical or boundary limits give trouble as regards divisions in support. Sometimes these seem to have been partly within and partly outside the limits. Where there is a probable claim this has been noted.

The chronological or time limits give no licence, and it is perhaps a little hard on some units that did some very severe fighting on one or more days before or after a recognised battle that they should be excluded. Particularly hard cases seem to be those of the 50th, 61st and 66th in connection with the fighting in the region of the Avre and Luce valleys, 28th–30th March, 1918, when these and other divisions by their splendid efforts prevented the line from being broken, and that after they had long passed all credible limits of endurance. The Battle of Rosières is given the dates 26th and 27th March, and that of the Avre, 4th April, by which latter date these three divisions were out of the line, the fighting 28th–30th March, south of the Somme, is thus outside both battles, although the despatch, in which these three divisions are mentioned, seems to give it an importance equal to that of the fighting on 4th April.

Again the Battle of the Somme, 1916, the Third Battle of Ypres, now the Battles of Ypres, 1917, and the First and Second Battles of the Somme, 1918, have each been sub-divided into a number of battles with fixed time limits; but in the course of these epic struggles certain divisions had intense fighting, with most serious losses, on days which are not within the dates of any of the recognised battles. For example, the 55th at the Somme, 1916, the 42nd and 47th at Ypres, 1917, and the 62nd at the Second Somme, 1918, all made big and costly endeavours on days outside the chronological boundaries of a recognised battle. No doubt they will get the general honour, such as " The Battles of Ypres, 1917," and have to be content with that.

The Committee have clearly taken great pains to arrive at sound principles, and to apply these wisely, and as they had every possible advantage in the way of information, their decisions, although in odd cases causing disappointment, will doubtless be accepted in the true soldiers' spirit.

In 1918 several Territorial divisions were practically destroyed, such as the 50th and 66th; these were during the last few months reconstituted, being made up largely with Regular or New Army battalions. Such divisions have been treated as Territorial to the end. If this is considered more than fair to the Territorial Force it is counterbalanced by the fact that some of the New Army Divisions, which had also been very hardly hit, such as the 34th, were, after the spring campaign of 1918, composed largely of Territorial battalions from Italy and Palestine.

The 25th has most handsomely admitted their good fortune in receiving seasoned battalions from Italy, including a brigade of the 48th.

42ND (EAST LANCASHIRE) DIVISION. First Line.

Defence of Egypt.		3–4 February, 1915.
The Battles of Helles, Dardanelles.	Second Battle of Krithia.	6–8 May, 1915.
	Third Battle of Krithia.	4 June, 1915.
Battle of Rumani, Egypt.		4–5 Aug., 1916.
The Battles of Ypres, 1917.	The Division was not mentioned in the despatch, but was in line from 1st to 18th September; it attacked on 6th and later dates. This was not one of the recognised battles.	
The First Battles of the Somme, 1918.	First Battle of Bapaume.	24–25 March, 1918.
	First Battle of Arras, 1918.	28 March, 1918.
	Battle of the Ancre, 1918.	5 April, 1918.
The Second Battles of the Somme, 1918	Battle of Albert, 1918	21–23 Aug., 1918.
	Second Battle of Bapaume.	31 Aug.–3 Sept., 1918.
The Battles of the Hindenburg Line.	Battle of the Canal du Nord.	27 Sept.–1 Oct., 1918.
The Final Advance.	Battle of the Selle.	17–25 Oct., 1918.
	Battle of the Sambre.	4 Nov., 1918.
	The Division was not engaged at the Battle of the Sambre on 4th November. It was in second line (see map, p. 294, Messrs. Dent's edition of despatches), but seems to have been within the official boundaries. It passed to front line on the 5th.	

APPENDIX

43RD (WESSEX) DIVISION. First Line. 44TH (HOME COUNTIES) DIVISION. First Line. 45TH (WESSEX) DIVISION. Second Line.

The Divisions went to India, were broken up, and were not in action as divisions.

46TH (NORTH MIDLAND) DIVISION. First Line.

Battle of Neuve Chapelle.   10–13 March, 1915.

The Battle of Loos   25 Sept.–8 Oct., 1915.
With "attack on Hohenzollern Redoubt, 13th October." The Division is mentioned in the despatch as attacking the redoubt on the 13th, but is not mentioned as attacking on 25th September. Their losses on the 13th were very heavy.

The Battles of the Somme, 1916.   Battle of Albert, 1916.   1–13 July, 1916.

Advance to Hindenburg Line, 1917.   March, 1917.
The Division was engaged on several occasions.

The Battles of Arras, 1917.   9 April–4 May, 1917.
With flanking operations towards Lens, 3 June–26 August. The Division was nearly ten weeks in the line and captured positions on 24 and 28 June.

Battle of Hill 70.   15–25 Aug., 1917.
Only part of the Division was engaged, the principal attack being by the Canadians on their right.

The Battles of the Hindenburg Line.   Battle of the St. Quentin Canal.   29 Sept.–2 Oct., 1918.

208 THE TERRITORIAL DIVISIONS

46TH (NORTH MIDLAND) DIVISION. First Line—*continued*

                Battle of the Beaurevoir Line.   3–5 Oct., 1918.

                Battle of Cambrai, 1918.   8–9 Oct., 1918.

The Final Advance. Battle of the Selle. 17–25 Oct., 1918.

                Battle of the Sambre. 4 Nov., 1918.

                The infantry was not heavily engaged on the 4th, but the Division was in second line (see map, p. 294), and was within boundaries. It " passed through " that night.

                47TH (SECOND LONDON) DIVISION. First Line

Battle of Festubert.   15–25 May, 1915.

The Battle of Loos.   25 Sept.–8 Oct., 1915.

The Battles of the Somme, 1916.   Battle of Flers-Courcelette.   15–22 Sept., 1916.

                Battle of the Transloy Ridges.   1–18 Oct., 1916.

The Battle of Messines, 1917.   7–14 June, 1917.

The Battles of Ypres, 1917.   31 July–10 Nov., 1917

                The 47th was not mentioned in the despatch, but took part in some attacks in latter half of August. It may not have been engaged in any of the recognised battles.

Battle of Cambrai, 1917.   20 Nov.–3 Dec., 1917.

APPENDIX

The First Battles of the Somme, 1918.	Battle of St. Quentin.	21–23 March, 1918.
	First Battle of Bapaume.	24–25 March, 1918.
	First Battle of Arras, 1918.	28 March, 1918.

The 47th might claim to have been in this battle. They were very close to the southern boundary, Authuille, but are not mentioned in the despatch. The fighting at the south of the line was not so intense as further north.

Battle of the Ancre.   5 April, 1918.

The despatch does not mention the units engaged, but the 47th was in the line and had very heavy fighting in this battle on 5th–6th April.

The Battle of Amiens.   8–11 Aug., 1918.

Not in despatch. Entered line on the 10th.

The Second Battles of the Somme, 1918.	Battle of Albert, 1918	21–23 Aug., 1918.
	Second Battle of Bapaume.	31 Aug.–3 Sept., 1918.

48TH (SOUTH MIDLAND) DIVISION.   First Line.

The Battles of the Somme, 1916.	*Battle of Albert, 1916.*	1–13 July, 1916.

The Division was in support.

	Battle of Bazentin Ridge.	14–17 July, 1916.
	Battle of Pozières Ridge.	23 July–3 Sept., 1916.

NOTE.—The 48th does not seem to have attacked in the Battles of Flers-Courcelette or the Transloy Ridges, but might have a claim, to the latter at least, as being within the boundaries. They were holding the line long after the "official" battle closed.

48TH (SOUTH MIDLAND) DIVISION. First Line—*continued*

Advance to the Hindenburg Line.	Occupation of Peonne, etc.	March, 1917.
The Battles of Ypres, 1917.	*Battle of Pilckem Ridge.*	31 July–2 Aug., 1917.
	The Division was in support.	
	Battle of Langemarck, 1917.	16–18 Aug., 1917.
	Battle of Broodseinde.	4 Oct., 1917.
	Battle of Poelcappelle.	9 Oct., 1917.
Italy.	Battle of the Piave (and Asiago Plateau).	15–24 June, 1918.
	Battle of Vittorio Veneto.	24 Oct.–4 Nov., 1918.

NOTE.—One brigade was with the 25th Division in the final advance in France and took the village of Beaurevoir in the battle of that name, 4th October, took a prominent part in the battle of the Selle, 18th October, and captured Landrecies in the Battle of the Sambre, 4th November.

49TH (WEST RIDING) DIVISION. First Line.

Battle of Aubers Ridge.		9th May, 1915.
	The Division was in support and held the line, while the 7th and 8th attacked.	
The Battles of the Somme, 1916.	Battle of Albert, 1916.	1–13 July, 1916.
	Battle of Bazentin Ridge.	14–17 July, 1916.
	Battle of Pozières Ridge.	23 July–3 Sept., 1916.

APPENDIX

	Battle of Thiepval Ridge.	26–28 Sept., 1916.

The 49th was on the Somme, Thiepval Front, from 30th June to the beginning of October. They did not attack in the Battle of Bazentin Ridge, but were in support and within the official boundary. Portions of the Division attacked in the Battles of Pozières and Thiepval.

The Battles of Ypres, 1917.	Battle of Poelcappelle.	9 Oct., 1917.

The Division was about the salient throughout the period of the Third Battle of Ypres, and although only mentioned in the despatch as attacking on 9th October, it may claim others of these battles as having been within the boundaries, particularly the two Passchendaele battles. Unfortunately their own history gives almost no guidance.

The Battles of the Lys.	*Battle of Estaires.*	9–11 April, 1918.

The Division was heavily engaged on 10th and 11th.

	Battle of Hazebrouck	12–15 April, 1918.
	Battle of Bailleul.	13–15 April, 1918.
	First Battle of Kemmel Ridge.	17–19 April, 1918.
	Second Battle of Kemmel Ridge.	25–26 April, 1918.
	Battle of the Scherpenberg.	29 April, 1918.

The Battles of the Hindenburg Line.	*Battle of Cambrai,* 1918, with pursuit to Selle.	8–12 Oct., 1918.

The Division was heavily engaged on 11th and 12th.

P

49TH (WEST RIDING) DIVISION. First Line—*continued*

The Final Advance.	Battle of Valenciennes.	1–2 Nov., 1918.
	NOTE.—Although the 49th was not attacking during the Battle of the Selle, 17th–25th October, or the Battle of the Sambre, 4th November, it may have a claim as having been within the boundaries. Part of the Division did remain in the front line between 2nd and 11th November.	

50TH (NORTHUMBRIAN) DIVISION. First Line.

The Battles of Ypres, 1915.	Battle of Gravenstafel Ridge.	22–23 April, 1915.
	In Sir John French's despatch, paragraph 4, he mentioned that he placed the 50th at the disposal of General Plumer on the night of the 22nd. A portion of the Division was within the boundary of the battle on the evening of the 23rd.	
	Battle of St. Julien.	24 April–4 May, 1915.
	Battle of Frezenberg Ridge.	8–13 May, 1915.
	Battle of Bellewaerde Ridge.	24–25 May, 1915.
The Battles of the Somme, 1916.	Battle of Flers-Courcelette.	15–22 Sept., 1916.
	Battle of Morval.	25–28 Sept., 1916.
	Battle of the Transloy Ridges.	1–18 Oct., 1916.
The Battles of Arras, 1917.	First Battle of the Scarpe, 1917.	9–14 April, 1917.
	Second Battle of the Scarpe, 1917.	23–24 April, 1917.
The Battles of Ypres, 1917.	*Second Battle of Passchendaele.*	26 Oct.–10 Nov., 1917.

APPENDIX 213

The First Battles of the Somme, 1918.	Battle of St. Quentin. 21–23 March, 1918. With actions for the Somme crossings, 24th–25th March. Battle of Rosières. 26–27 March, 1918. NOTE.—Paragraph 47 of the despatch shows that there was very heavy fighting in the Avre and Luce valleys on 29th, 30th and 31st March, in which the 50th was engaged, but the official list gives the Battle of the Avre one day only, the 4th April, and takes no notice of the battle 29th to 31st March.
The Battles of the Lys.	Battle of Estaires. 9–11 April, 1918. *Battle of Hazebrouck.* 12–15 April, 1918. The Division was still fighting on the 12th and 13th.
The Battle of the Aisne, 1918.	27 May–6 June, 1918.
The Battles of the Hindenburg Line.	Battle of Beaurevoir Line. 3–5 Oct., 1918. Battle of Cambrai, 1918. 8–9 Oct., 1918. See map, p. 287, Messrs. Dent's edition.
The Final Advance.	Battle of the Selle. 17–25 Oct., 1918. Battle of the Sambre. 4 Nov., 1918.

51ST (HIGHLAND) DIVISION. First Line.

The Battles of the Somme, 1916.	Battle of Bazentin Ridge. 14–17 July, 1916. And "subsequent attack on High Wood," 20th–25th July. The Division is not mentioned as engaged in the British attack, 14th–17th July, but is stated in the despatch to have

51ST (HIGHLAND) DIVISION. First Line—*continued*

	repulsed an attack at High Wood on the 24th.	
	Battle of the Ancre, 1916 (Beaumont Hamel).	13–18 Nov., 1916.
The Battles of Arras, 1917.	First Battle of the Scarpe, 1917.	9–14 April, 1917.
	Second Battle of the Scarpe, 1917.	23–24 April, 1917.
	Third Battle of the Scarpe, 1917.	3–4 May, 1917.
	And " capture of Rœux, 13th–14th."	
The Battles of Ypres, 1917.	Battle of Pilckem Ridge.	31 July–2 Aug., 1918.
	Battle of Menin Road Ridge.	20–25 Sept., 1917.
Battle of Cambrai, 1917.		20 Nov.–3 Dec., 1917.
The First Battles of the Somme, 1918.	Battle of St. Quentin.	21–23 March, 1918.
	First Battle of Bapaume.	24–25 March, 1918.
	The Division is not referred to in the despatch, but was still fighting hard on the 24th–25th as rearguard.	
The Battles of the Lys.	Battle of Estaires.	9–11 April, 1918.
	Battle of Hazebrouck.	12–15 April, 1918.
The Battles of the Marne, 1918.	Battle of Tardenois (Ardre Valley).	20–31 July, 1918.
The Second Battles of Arras, 1918.	Battle of the Scarpe, 1918.	26–30 Aug., 1918.

APPENDIX 215

The Battles of the Hindenburg Line.	*Battle of Cambrai, 1918, and pursuit to the Selle.* 8-12 Oct., 1918.
	The Division captured several positions on the 12th, after stiff fighting.
The Final Advance.	Battle of the Selle. 17-25 Oct., 1918.
	Battle of Valenciennes and capture of Mount Houy. 1-2 Nov., 1918.
	The Division was not in the first line on the 1st-2nd November, but attacked and captured a portion of Mount Houy on 28th October. The time limit may exclude its claim.

52ND (LOWLAND) DIVISION. First Line.

The Battles of Helles.	Third Battle of Krithia. 4 June, 1915. With subsequent actions.
	NOTE.—The Division did not land in time for the battle of 4th June, but, as narrated in the despatch, took part in several fiercely contested actions, mentioned in the Official List subsequent to that date, when they had very heavy losses.
Egypt.	Battle of Rumani. 4-5 Aug., 1916.
The Invasion of Palestine.	First Battle of Gaza. 26-27 March, 1917.
	Second Battle of Gaza. 17-19 April, 1917.
	Third Battle of Gaza. 27 Oct.-7 Nov., 1917.
	Battle of Nebi Samwil. 17-24 Nov., 1917.
	Battle of Jaffa. 21-22 Dec., 1917.

52ND (LOWLAND) DIVISION. First Line—*continued*

The Second Battles of Arras, 1918.	Battle of Albert.	21–23 Aug., 1918.
	Battle of the Scarpe, 1918.	26–30 Aug., 1918.
	Battle of the Drocourt-Quéant Line.	2–3 Sept., 1918.
The Battles of the Hindenburg Line.	Battle of the Canal du Nord.	27 Sept.–1 Oct., 1918.

53RD (WELSH) DIVISION. First Line.

The Battles of Suvla, Dardanelles.	The Landing at Suvla.	6–15 Aug., 1915.
	Battle of Scimitar Hill.	21 Aug., 1915.
Egypt.	Battle of Rumani.	4–5 Aug., 1916.
The Invasion of Palestine.	First Battle of Gaza.	26–27 March, 1917.
	Second Battle of Gaza.	17–19 April, 1917.
	Third Battle of Gaza.	27 Oct.–7 Nov., 1917.
	Defence of Jerusalem.	26–30 Dec., 1917.
The Battles of Megiddo.	Battle of Sharon.	19–25 Sept., 1918.
	Battle of Nablus.	19–25 Sept., 1918.

54TH (EAST ANGLIAN) DIVISION. First Line.

The Battles of Suvla, Dardanelles.	The Landing at Suvla.	6–15 Aug., 1915.
	Battle of Scimitar Hill.	21st Aug., 1915.

APPENDIX

The Invasion of Palestine.	First Battle of Gaza.	26–27 March, 1917.
	Second Battle of Gaza.	17–19 April, 1917.
	Third Battle of Gaza.	27 Oct.–7 Nov., 1917.
	Battle of Nebi Samwil	17–24 Nov., 1917.
	Battle of Jaffa.	21–22 Dec., 1917.
The Battles of Megiddo.	Battle of Sharon.	19–25 Sept., 1918.
	Battle of Nablus.	19–25 Sept., 1918.

55TH (WEST LANCASHIRE) DIVISION. First Line.

The Battles of the Somme, 1916.	*Battle of Ginchy.*	9 Sept., 1916.
	The Division is not referred to in the despatch as attacking on the 9th Sept. According to the *History of the 55th* they attacked at Guillemont on 8th August, during the period of the fighting at Delville Wood, but the locus of that battle is the wood, and they also attacked at Ginchy on the 9th September.	
	Battle of Morval.	25–28 Sept., 1916.
The Battles of Ypres, 1917.	Battle of Pilckem Ridge.	31 July–2 Aug., 1917.
	Battle of the Menin Road Ridge.	20–25 Sept., 1917.
Battle of Cambrai, 1917.		20 Nov.–3 Dec., 1917.
The Battles of the Lys.	Battle of Estaires and First Defence of Givenchy.	9–11 April, 1918.
	Battle of Hazebrouck.	12–15 April, 1918.
	The Division was not relieved till the 15th, and had some hard fighting on the 12th and 13th, *see* Sir D. Haig's special order.	

THE TERRITORIAL DIVISIONS

56TH (FIRST LONDON) DIVISION. First Line.

The Battles of the Somme, 1916.	Battle of Albert, 1916.	1-13 July, 1916.
	Battle of Ginchy.	9 Sept., 1916.
	Battle of Flers-Courcelette.	15-22 Sept., 1916.
	Battle of Morval.	25-28 Sept., 1916.
	Battle of the Transloy Ridges.	1-18 Oct., 1916.

The 56th was one of the attacking divisions on 26th September near Combles, and on 7th–8th Oct. further north.

The Battles of Arras, 1917.	First Battle of the Scarpe, 1917.	9-14 April, 1917.
	Third Battle of the Scarpe, 1917.	3-4 May, 1917.

The Division attacked on the 3rd, and is mentioned in the despatch as capturing a position on the 11th.

The Battles of Ypres, 1917.	Battle of Langemarck, 1917.	16-18 Aug., 1917.

The Battle of Cambrai 1917.		20 Nov.-3 Dec., 1917.

The First Battles of the Somme, 1918.	First Battle of Arras, 1918.	28 March, 1918.

The Second Battles of the Somme, 1918.	Battle of Albert, 1918.	21-23 Aug., 1918.

The Second Battles of Arras, 1918.	Battle of the Scarpe, 1918.	26-30 Aug., 1918.
	See Sir D. Haig's telegram of 13th Sept.	
	Battle of the Drocourt-Quéant Line.	2-3 Sept., 1918.

APPENDIX

The Battles of the Hindenburg Line.	Battle of the Canal du Nord.	27 Sept.–1 Oct., 1918.
	Battle of Cambrai, with pursuit to the Selle.	8–12 Oct., 1918.
	The Division attacked and took positions on the 11th and 12th.	
The Final Advance.	*Battle of Valenciennes,* 1–2 Nov., 1918.	
	Although the 56th did not attack on the 1st or 2nd, they entered the line on the night of the 2nd, and have a claim as being within the official boundaries.	
	Battle of the Sambre. 4 Nov., 1918.	

57TH (WEST LANCASHIRE) DIVISION. Second Line.

The Battles of Ypres, 1917.	*Second Battle of Passchendaele.*	26 Oct.–10 Nov., 1917
	The Division is not referred to in the despatch, but as part of the XIVth Corps they attacked on 26th October.	
The Battles of the Lys.	*Battle of Hazebrouck.* 12–15 April, 1918.	
	Part of the Division was engaged.	
The Second Battles of Arras, 1918.	Battle of the Scarpe, 1918.	26–30 Aug., 1918.
	Battle of the Drocourt-Quéant Line.	2–3 Sept., 1918.
The Battles of the Hindenburg Line.	Battle of the Canal du Nord.	27 Sept.–1 Oct., 1918.
	Battle of Cambrai, 1918.	8–9 Oct., 1918.

58TH (FIRST LONDON) DIVISION. Second Line.

The Advance to the Hindenburg Line, 1917.		March, 1917.
The Battles of Arras, 1917.	Battle of Bullecourt. 3–17 May, 1917.	

THE TERRITORIAL DIVISIONS

58TH (FIRST LONDON) DIVISION. Second Line—*continued*

The Battles of Ypres, 1917.	Battle of the Menin Road Ridge.	20–25 Sept., 1917.
	Battle of Polygon Wood.	26 Sept.–3 Oct., 1917.
	Second Battle of Passchendaele.	26 Oct.–10 Nov., 1917.
The First Battles of the Somme, 1918.	Battle of St. Quentin.	21–23 March, 1918.
	Battle of the Ancre, 1918. 5th April with subsequent action of *Villers Bretonneux*.	24–25 April, 1918.

The Division was on the south flank and had rather heavy losses about the 24th–25th.

The Battle of Amiens.   8–11 Aug., 1918.

The Second Battles of the Somme, 1918.   *Battle of Albert*, 1918. 21–23 Aug., 1918. As part of the III. Corps they entered the front line on the 22nd.

Second Battle of Bapaume.   31 Aug.–3 Sept., 1918.

The Battles of the Hindenburg Line.   Battle of Epéhy.   18 Sept., 1918.

59TH (NORTH MIDLAND) DIVISION. Second Line.

The Advance to the Hindenburg Line, 1917.   March, 1917.

The Battles of Ypres, 1917.   Battle of Polygon Wood.   26 Sept.–3 Oct., 1917.

Battle of Cambrai, 1917.   20 Nov.–3 Dec., 1917.

See map in Messrs. Dent's Edition.

APPENDIX 221

The First Battles of the Somme, 1918.	Battle of St. Quentin. 21–23 March, 1918. See map in Messrs. Dent's edition.	
	One brigade was engaged in the First Battle of Bapaume.	24–25 March, 1918.
The Battles of the Lys.	*Battle of Bailleul.* 13–15 April, 1918. At this period the Division was much split up, and parts of it were in others of the Lys battles.	

60TH (SECOND LONDON) DIVISION. Second Line.

Macedonia.	*Battle of Doiran*, 1917.	24–25 April, and 8–9 May, 1917.
The Invasion of Palestine.	Third Battle of Gaza.	27 Oct.–7 Nov., 1917.
	Battle of Nebi Samwil.	17–24 Nov., 1917.
	Defence of Jerusalem and numerous subsequent actions, January to July, 1918.	26–30 Dec., 1917.
The Battles of Megiddo.	Battle of Sharon.	19–25 Sept., 1918.
	Battle of Nablus.	19–25 Sept., 1918.

61ST (SOUTH MIDLAND) DIVISION. Second Line.

The Battles of the Somme, 1916.		14–17 July, 1916.
	The Division took part in an attack at Fromelles, 19th–20th July, 1916, which in the Official List was stated to be subsidiary to the Battle of Bazentin Ridge.	
Advance to Hindenburg Line, 1917.	Capture of Bapaume and Chaulnes.	March, 1917.

222 THE TERRITORIAL DIVISIONS

61ST (SOUTH MIDLAND) DIVISION. Second Line—*continued*

The Battles of Ypres, 1917.
The Division is not mentioned in the despatch, but was engaged at Ypres on various dates in the latter half of August and first week of September. These were not perhaps within the limits of "recognised battles."

Battle of Cambrai, 1917.
20 Nov.–3 Dec., 1917.
Mentioned in the despatch as assembling, took over from the 12th Division about 1st December, and had stiff fighting for several days.

The First Battles of the Somme, 1918.
Battle of St. Quentin 21–23 March, 1918. And actions for Somme crossings, 24th and 25th March.
Battle of Rosières. 26–27 March, 1918.

The Battles of the Lys.
Battle of Hazebrouck. 12–15 April, 1918.
Battle of Béthune. 18 April, 1918.

The Final Advance.
Battle of the Selle. 17–25 Oct., 1918.
Battle of Valenciennes. 1–2 Nov., 1918.
Battle of the Sambre. 4 Nov., 1918.
The Division left the front line on the 2nd, but appears to have remained within the official boundaries.

62ND (WEST RIDING) DIVISION. Second Line.

The Advance to the Hindenburg Line, 1917.
March, 1917.

The Battles of Arras, 1917.
Battle of Bullecourt. 3–17 May, 1917.

APPENDIX 223

Battle of Cambrai, 1917.	20 Nov.–3 Dec., 1917.

The First Battles of the Somme, 1918.	*First Battle of Bapaume.* 24–25 March, 1918.
	The Division was in action on the afternoon and evening of the 25th.
	First Battle of Arras, 1918. 28 March, 1918.

The Battles of the Marne, 1918.	Battle of Tardenois (Ardre valley). 20–31 July, 1918.

The Second Battles of the Somme, 1918.	Second Battle of Bapaume. 31 Aug.–3 Sept., 1918.
	The Division had hard fighting on 25–27 August, but these dates do not fall within the time limits of either of the battles of Albert, 21–23 August, or of Bapaume.

The Battles of the Hindenburg Line.	Battle of Havrincourt. 12 Sept., 1918.
	Battle of the Canal du Nord. 27 Sept.–1 Oct., 1918.
	See map, p. 280, Messrs. Dent's edition. The 62nd passed through the 3rd on the 27th, continued the attack, and captured Marcoing, etc.

The Final Advance.	Battle of the Selle. 17–25 Oct., 1918.
	Battle of the Sambre. 4 Nov., 1918.
	NOTE.—The Division was not in the front line during the Battle of Cambrai, 8th–9th October, 1918, but other divisions of the VI Corps were engaged and part at least of the 62nd may have been within the official boundaries.

224 THE TERRITORIAL DIVISIONS

66TH (EAST LANCASHIRE) DIVISION. Second Line.

The Battles of Ypres, 1917.	Battle of Poelcappelle. 9 Oct., 1917.
The First Battles of the Somme, 1918.	Battle of St. Quentin. 21–23 March, 1918. With actions for Somme crossings, 24th–25th March.
	Battle of Rosières. 26–27 March, 1918.
	Battle of the Avre. 4 April, 1918.
	Para. 47 of the despatch shows that the 66th was in the heavy fighting, 28th–31st March, in the Avre and Luce valleys, when they made counter-attacks; it is not said they were fighting on 4th April. The Official List makes no reference to the fighting 28th–31st March in this neighbourhood.
The Battles of the Hindenburg Line.	Battle of Cambrai, 1918. 8–9 Oct., 1918.
The Final Advance.	Battle of the Selle. 17–25 Oct., 1918.
	Battle of the Sambre. 4 Nov., 1918.
	The map, p. 294, Messrs. Dent's edition, shows the 66th in support to the north-east of Le Cateau. It would thus be within the official boundary.
	In regard to the Battle of the Beaurevoir Line, 3rd–5th October, the divisions of the XIII. Corps in the front line were the 25th and 50th. The 66th was in reserve and it is not clear that it was within the official limits, although certainly close thereto.

www.ingramcontent.com/pod-product-compliance
Lightning Source LLC
Chambersburg PA
CBHW070841160426
43192CB00012B/2268